When Life Kicks
KICK BACK

Tamara Hell

When Life Kicks

KICK
BACK

**Survival
Lessons
For
Personal
Crisis
&
Life's
Challenges**

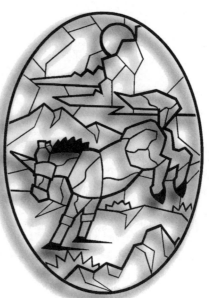

Tamara Hall

Communications Plus

Communications Plus, 6734 Gooch Hill Road, Bozeman, MT 59718

06 05 04 03 02
Sixth printing, 2003

The events in this book actually did occur, but the names and, in some
cases, the locations have been changed to protect the identities of the
people involved.

The Glory Of Love
Words and Music by Billy Hill
Copyright © 1936 Shapiro, Bernstein & Co., Inc., New York
Copyright Renewed
International Copyright Secured All Rights Reserved
Used by Permission

Edited by Phyllis Rigg
Cover illustration by Chris England
Cover design by Chris England and Michael Dougherty

Hall, Tamara, 1949-
      When Life Kicks, Kick Back: Survival Lessons
for Personal Crisis and Life's Challenges/Tamara
Hall, - 1st ed.
      p. cm.
1. Parenting 2. Abuse 3. Self-Esteem I. Hall,
Tamara II. Title
                              96-096932

ISBN 0-9653683-0-0 (paperback)

To Kelly

My beloved
My friend

Song of Solomon

Acknowledgements

This book became a reality because of the following people who offered encouragement, technical advice, marketing ideas and wisdom. They are my angels.

Kelly Hall, Tera Hall, Tiffani and Shane Coleman, Troy Hall, Stacy Juhnke, Phyllis, Tom, and Julianna Rigg, Laurie and John Shadoan, Molly and Bob Macdonald, Faith and Jack Dredla, Elli Hawks, Phil and Connie Olsen, Dorthy Dacar, Kathy Shaw, Jim and Jan Schwartz, Shirley and George DeBelly, Vallia Young, Dara Lynn Arnold, Shane and Beverly Montalban, Judy Hall, Val Heath, Pat Noel, The Country Bookshelf, Bozeman, MT., and Type and Graphics, Bozeman, MT.

Contents

When Life Kicks—Kick Back

Stained Glass Windows

No One Gets Out Of This Life Without Hurting

Everyone experiences emotional and physical pain. We are all the walking wounded.

My mother used to say, "Tamara, if a group of friends got together and put their problems in the middle of the room, they would study the pile and take their own problems back." When I was young, I thought, "Mother, you need nicer friends." Now, I know she was right.

Your current crisis may be a health trauma, a relationship break-up, a parenting nightmare, a job change or the death of a loved one. Perhaps a family member or friend is fighting addiction or depression. Whatever the circumstance, people hurt because life hurts.

We are all like intricate stained-glass windows. Each experience in our lives forms one section of a unique picture. Some pieces are bright, attractive and distinct. Some pieces are muted, dark and distorted. Eventually, all of our pieces fit together to form a perfect whole.

But, the window, no matter how beautiful, does not come to life until it is illuminated. That illumination is a union of many sources. It is an understanding of our past. It is the discernment of our unique gifts. It is the friendship, nurturing, and kindness of others. It is the acknowledgement that we cannot control all that happens to us. It is tolerance and appreciation of others. It is realizing that we are responsible for the choices we make. Finally, the force that creates and binds all the sources of illumination together is the ever-present power and love of God.

This book is my window, the pieces and the patterns. My window is not more unique than yours. It is certainly not more beautiful. I share my story with you in the humble hope that your window will be enhanced by the sharing.

Reaching Out

The purpose of this book is to show all of us that life's most difficult trials teach us survival lessons that prepare us for future adversity. Throughout, I will share the challenges I have experienced in my life, the messages I have received and the lessons I have learned. It goes without saying that my life challenges pale when compared with many people. I cannot, however, tell their stories. I can only tell mine.

Writing this book has been an emotional and creative challenge. It is always difficult to disclose thoughts, fears and hopes. There is a vulnerability that accompanies self-disclosure. Reaching out to you in this book is a risk. If, however, we do not reach out and share with others, we do not grow.

This book is divided into three parts. Each part helps reveal the pieces of my stained glass window and shed light on it, so that my pattern is revealed. The three sections and their corresponding chapters are as follows:

- ❋ PART ONE–Survival Lessons–Stepping Back (Chapters 1–7)

- ❋ PART TWO–Survival Lessons–Stepping Forward (Chapters 8–9)

- ❋ PART THREE–The Final Lesson (Chapter 10)

PART ONE—Survival Lessons—Stepping Back

Part One discloses adversities I faced as a child. It looks at survival lessons that I have learned from past crises. These are the darkest pieces of my window, but they are only pieces, not the whole. They influenced me. They do not define me. Part One ends with the story of my husband, Kelly. He was the beginning of my learning to love myself and represents some of my brightest pieces.

Most authors tell their personal stories in first person. I chose to break that paradigm in Part One of this book and tell the stories of my childhood in the third person. I did this to make the strong point that once we survive adversity we must stand back and ask, "What lessons has this crisis taught me?"

There is a risk in telling personal stories in the third person. Some people will accuse me of disassociating myself from the painful emotions of my formative years. I assure you, that is not the case. The first step in personal growth is to re-visit and re-open painful wounds from our past. I have analyzed my childhood memories. I have re-lived the pain. I have worked hard to understand the child I was and the child I am.

In order to write this book, I had to vividly recall many of the most traumatic experiences of childhood. After all, the memories could not be accurately recorded on paper if they did not first travel through my heart. At times, the revival of childhood memories would wrap me in such a heavy blanket

3

of fear and sadness that I would have to stop writing and take a walk. I would pray and remind myself that the past is the past and can no longer hurt me.

The re-experiencing of painful memories is only the first step, however. We cannot heal and grow unless we move beyond the pain of our past. Otherwise, we become victims trapped in self-pity and fear. We all know people who have sacrificed the opportunity of today and the hope of tomorrow by obsessing on the pain of yesterday.

Each of us has experienced great suffering and injustice, but we are survivors. I have chosen to tell the stories of my youth in the third person to encourage you to stand back from your toughest experiences and look at them from a new perspective.

Once I decided the format that I would use in the telling of my lessons, I had to decide which events I should relate to you. This created a unique challenge. I asked the obvious questions–"Will the reader find this situation interesting?, Will this lesson help others?, and Does the telling of this incident enhance the book?" The most important criterion for inclusion, however, was "Does the telling of this story needlessly hurt another person?" There were stories that did not make the final edit because when I turned to God for guidance, He convicted me that they were indeed hurtful. To be honest, it was hard to delete some of those dramatic chapters. But, in each case, God showed me another experience from my past that better illustrated the lesson.

PART TWO—Survival Lessons—Stepping Forward

Part Two tells of the on-going challenges I face as an adult. It is the part of my stained glass window that deals with lessons

4

I am currently learning. These stories are less dark than the tragedies of my childhood. After all, I have more power and choices as an adult than I did as a child, when my world was dictated by the adults around me. However, they are difficult because they are often unending and, therefore, teach different lessons.

PART THREE—The Final Lesson

Part three is a myth—a composite of the lessons and messages that has made my survival from each crisis and challenge a reality.

It is my sincere prayer that in this parable you will discover the guidance and power that helps you kick back when life kicks.

When Life Kicks—Kick Back

PART ONE

Survival Lessons—Stepping Back

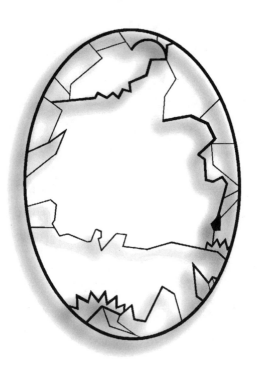

Chapter One
Messages

Tamara at Two

The scorching sun burned through the windshield. The car was hot. There was no relief in sight. Kay and her mother, Doris (who was referred to as Porky by everyone), sat in silence. Kay's two small children wrestled in the back seat. They were hours into the long cross-country trek from Edmonton to Toronto.

Kay had been in a foul mood long before the black, endless asphalt darkened her outlook. She was angry at her husband, Joe. They were both hopelessly stubborn and short-tempered. Kay and Joe were as volatile together as gasoline and matches. Every small battle escalated into a war.

"I hate him," Kay grumbled.

"You don't hate him," Porky's gentle voice insisted. "It would be easier if you did. You two should never have gotten married. You're too much alike. I am glad you decided to leave him."

"It isn't permanent. I'm just trying to scare him."

"Oh, Kay, you can't change him."

"But, I can't leave him. I have two kids, and I'm pregnant."

"You two will kill each other if you stay together," Porky mumbled.

Screams from the two toddlers in the back seat made further discussion impossible.

"You two stop fighting right now, or I am going to spank you!" Kay shouted.

Oh Kay," pleaded Porky, "they're just babies."

"They aren't babies."

"You must admit it has been a long day for them. Maybe we should find a hotel."

"I don't want to stop. It'll be cooler if we drive at night."

Kay turned her head to the back seat and threatened, "You two lay down and be quiet. I'm serious. I will spank you!" Finally the darkness and heat overtook the two children, and they drifted off to sleep.

"Kay, there are lights up ahead. Let's stop for the night."

"No, we aren't stopping, but I could use a cup of coffee."

Kay pulled off the exit and found a drive-in. After a short wait the young girl approached the car.

"What can I get you?"

"Shhh . . . ," warned Kay, pointing to the children in the back seat. "Don't wake them. We'll have one cup of strong coffee and a cup of tea."

"Anything else?" the girl asked in a hushed tone.

"No, that's all."

Suddenly Kay felt a small hand on the side of her face. With surprising strength, her two-and a half-year-old daughter,

Tamara, pushed her mother's head aside and announced in a voice riddled with authority, "Lady, me want a hot dog." Porky burst out laughing. The young waitress joined in.

"Stop laughing," snapped Kay. "You'll just encourage her."

"Oh, Kay, how can you get mad. She is such a live wire."

"She's obstinate and exhausting–she makes my life so difficult."

"Stop it, Kay!" warned Porky. "She will hear you."

It was too late. The child had heard her mother. The message had been sent and received.

A clouded piece of the window was put into place.

Tamara at Fifteen

The fifteen-year-old girl's breath made a small fog on the cold glass of the car window. With her finger, she wrote the one word that best described her pain–*ALONE*. She breathed harder and added the words, *I DON'T CARE*. She shook her head as she realized the words were not accurate. She erased the word *I* and whispered cynically to herself, "That's better, Tamara. *DON'T CARE*, then you'll be safe." Kay's words shattered her daughter's self-indulgent anger.

"Only two more hours, and we'll be there."

"Only two hours of freedom left, and I'm stuck in a car with my mother. Do I get a last meal?"

"Don't be so dramatic, Tamara. Freedom–last meal–you aren't going to prison, only a private girls' school."

"You seem to forget, Mother, this is the second time you've sent me away. I know a prison when I hear it," Tamara sneered.

"It's a finishing school."

"It's a prison. I'm being exiled at fifteen."

"Stop it, Tamara. I refuse to argue with you today. This is the best thing for you."

"You mean, it is the best thing for you!"

"That's not true. You and I both need this break from each other."

"I bet Father doesn't want me to . . ."

"Your father and I agree that this will be good for you."

"You and Father agreeing. Now, there's a first."

Kay's tone reflected an exhaustion of patience, "Stop it! Your father and I have some things to work out, and we don't need the extra stress of your rebellious outbursts. I said I wouldn't fight with you today, and I won't, so quit trying to upset me." Silence overcame Tamara, and she drifted off to sleep.

"Tamara, wake up, and help me find the Frontage Road exit." Large green highway signs came into view. Tamara pointed and said, "There it is." They took the next turn-off and drove onto a gravel, two-lane road. As the road became rougher, the spaces between the farm houses lengthened.

"God, this place is in the boonies," Tamara grumbled.

"Don't swear! And, it isn't in the boonies. It has a nice country setting and . . ."

"Oh, please, Mother, you sound like a travel brochure."

"Stop getting smart with me," Kay warned.

As the car emerged over a small hill, a large stone fortress came into view.

"Oh my God," exclaimed Tamara, "it is a converted prison!"

"It's a restored fort. It's supposed to have one of the most beautiful chapels in the country."

"Oh, great. I suppose I'll be spending half my time in there asking for forgiveness."

"That certainly wouldn't hurt you. You'd better make the best of this young lady, or it's going to be a very long year."

The building was truly ominous. The landscape was flat and bare. A high wall encircled the grayish brown structure of crumbling stone. The contrast of architecture was somewhat disturbing. New additions had been added to the main building with little concern for consistency of form. They entered through an iron gate and stopped in front of heavy glass doors. Tamara jumped from the car and began unloading suitcases from the back seat.

"Why don't we look around before we unpack?" asked Kay.

"Thanks for the generous offer, but you better just drop me off and head back. I'm sure you have some important social engagement waiting for you."

Kay started to respond and then changed her mind. *Ignore her,* she said to herself. *Just a little while longer, and you'll be free of her for a year.* Kay smiled and walked towards the entry.

The nun who met them was dressed in a traditional long black robe with a large square headpiece framing her face. Tamara noticed that this nun possessed the same cold stare and unchallenged authority she had encountered in other nuns. *That must be from the universal code of nun behavior,* Tamara snickered to herself.

The nun lead them to a large dorm room.

"You will share this room with five girls."

"You put a real premium on privacy around here," Tamara interjected.

Kay glared at her daughter.

"Doors are to remain open at all times except when dressing. WE close the doors for dressing."

". . . and bathing," Tamara interrupted. "WE do have indoor plumbing, don't WE?"

"Of course we have indoor plumbing. This is one of the finest facilities for young women in the Northwest," the nun answered with controlled anger.

"What about my clothes? That closet is too small for six girls." said an unimpressed Tamara.

"It is perfectly adequate for the two dresses and one pair of slacks you are allowed to keep. And, of course, your uniforms don't take much space."

"Uniforms," Tamara shouted. "You can't be serious."

"Oh, yes, I am very serious," replied the smirking nun. "They are quite attractive–plaid skirts, white blouses, black blazer and knee socks."

"Oh my God, uniforms!" Tamara whispered.

"We do not swear here, Tamara. Ever! I suggest you remember that. Now, your mother may help you unpack and then she will join me in my office, so we can confirm the financial arrangements."

"I don't need your help," Tamara growled at Kay.

"But, I want to help you unpack . . .."

"Forget it. Besides, this isn't a place where people get what they want," Tamara snapped.

"You change your tone right now! Say good-bye to your mother," Sister Ruth demanded, obviously tired of Tamara's insolence.

"Good-bye, Mother. Don't miss me too terribly," Tamara replied in a voice reeking of sarcasm.

Kay took a step towards her daughter.

"Let's not fight," Kay softly pleaded.

"Just leave Mother. You'd better go pay these people for taking me off your hands."

And, with all the vehemence Tamara could muster, she turned and nodded towards the nun.

"Go with HER . . . NOW!"

The nun stopped and spun around.

"I have a name. It is Sister Ruth. When you refer to me, use my name. Not 'her,' not 'she,' but Sister Ruth. Do you understand?"

Tamara refused to acknowledge the nun's warning and, once again, bid a bitter farewell to Kay.

"Good-bye, Mother. I will see you in a year, unless I get time off for good behavior."

Kay followed the nun out of the room. Tamara walked to the window. The sun had set and a thin coating of ice was forming. Tamara scratched into the ice with her fingernail, *DON'T CARE.* Then, she slowly sank to the hard floor, pulled herself into a ball, and began to cry quietly.

A dark piece of glass was added to the window.

The Lesson

Children as Computers

t is obvious, that at age two, I was a vivacious, confident child who did not hesitate to express her needs. By fifteen, I was an angry teenager brimming with hostility and cynicism and determined to need no one.

My parents sent me to two different boarding schools, one in Canada when I was thirteen and one in North Dakota when I was fifteen. Both times I experienced fear and abandonment. In Canada, those feelings surfaced as depression. In North Dakota, they surfaced as anger.

I was always a strong-willed child, but I wasn't born with hostility and anger. How did it develop? How did I go from a trusting, vulnerable infant to a rebellious, embittered teenager in fifteen short years?

The answer is simple. Children are incredibly moldable. Each child's self-concept is a clean slate waiting to be written upon. Children trust. They expose their blank self-esteem to those who would define them, often with indelible ink.

If adults hold children close and whisper, "You are a precious package, and I will love you forever," the innocent souls rejoice and say, "Oh, yes, you know everything, and you are right." If adults push children away and growl, "You are unacceptable and unwanted," the innocent souls cry out, "Oh, yes, you know everything, and you are right."

A child is much like a computer because he builds each program on the original data. If a computer is programmed that "2 + 2 = 5," the most sophisticated spreadsheet will be forever flawed, because layer upon layer of accurate information will be distorted by the original false data that "2 + 2 = 5."

And, so it is with children. Competent counselors, patient partners, and tolerant teachers can enter positive messages, but those messages will be forever distorted, until the original flawed data is discovered and erased.

A look back at my formative years reveals a discernable path from an energetic, trusting infant to an aggressive, hostile teenager. The road that I traveled on during those first fifteen years was filled with many potholes–difficult challenges and negative messages. Many times I was implanted with false messages regarding my self-worth and potential. The messages I received were strong:

> You make life hard.

> You are different.

> We don't know what to do with you.

> We don't want you around.

Those false messages did not destroy my stained glass window, but they did dull some of the brightest colors and conceal some of the most delightful pieces.

Have you ever caught yourself irrationally reacting to a difficult situation and wondering, "Where did that response come from?" More than likely, the response was planted decades ago when you were a child. A destructive message implanted in a child must be erased or revised before the person can become complete.

Each time we correct a false message, we polish the glass in our windows. It is in the cleaning away of the grime that we allow the beauty and uniqueness of our window to illuminate us and those around us.

If you want to reach your full potential and survive life's tough times, you must separate the real from the flawed. You must ask yourself the following questions:

- ✸ "What negative voices whisper from my sub-conscious?"
- ✸ "What has been programmed into my computer?"

You must realize that these are false messages and consciously push the erase button every time they appear on the screen!

Chapter Two
Born Strong

School

Tamara rushed into the house with all the speed her six-year-old legs could muster and headed for the bathroom.

"Don't slam that door!" shouted Kay. "You'll wake your baby sister."

Kay was curled in a chair, lost in a romance novel. It was her favorite escape from the pressures of life. The living room was dark. The curtains were drawn tight, cutting off all signs of daylight.

The phone rang. Kay barely had the energy to get out of the big chair. She unwrapped her long legs, walked to the kitchen and lifted the receiver on the fifth ring.

"Hello, this is Kay."

"Are you Tamara's mother?" asked the caller.

"Yes, I am," Kay sighed. "What has she done now?"

"I am the principal of Tamara's school. Are you aware that your daughter has left first grade one hour early every day this week? It seems she doesn't return after afternoon recess."

"Oh, I am so sorry. She told me she was getting out early."

"And, you believed her?" It was impossible to miss the incredulous tone in the woman's voice.

"I thought it was possible, with it being the first week of school and all," Kay responded defensively. "I'll talk to her. I can assure you, it won't happen again."

Kay slammed down the phone and yelled, "Tamara, get in here right now." The child skipped into the kitchen with the same energy that carried her everywhere.

"Do you know who that was on the phone? It was your principal. She said you have been leaving school after recess. Is that true?"

Tamara could tell by her mother's tone she was in trouble, again.

"Yes," she mumbled.

"And, why would you do such a bad thing?"

"Because I get tired and it is hot and boring and I have to go to the bathroom and if you go during recess, there isn't time to play. And after recess, you can't go, so I just come home and go," Tamara explained in rapid fire succession.

"Well, you can't do that. First grade goes 'til three thirty."

"Three thirty!!" Tamara's voice was full of disbelief.

"That's right, three thirty—every day."

"Every day?" Tamara exclaimed, as shock crossed her face.

"That's right, three thirty. Only you will be staying until four all next week as punishment for leaving early."

Tamara put her hands on her hips, stomped the ground twice and announced, "Well, I can certainly tell I am not going to like first grade." She turned around and marched out of the room.

Tamara spent most of first grade in a public school. Then the parish priest convinced Kay to send Tamara and her older brother to a parochial school. It was expensive, but Joe insisted, "It will be good for them. They are spoiled. They need more discipline–especially Tamara. She is much too bull-headed."

Tamara was full of apprehension the day her mother drove them to the new Catholic school. "What will this school be like?," Tamara asked. "Just like your old one. All schools are the same," Kay answered in a matter-of-fact tone. But, it wasn't the same. A stern nun met her at the door and announced, "I am Sister Margaret. I will be your teacher. Follow me."

Sister turned so abruptly that the heel of her black shoe squeaked against the floor. Tamara was enthralled by the noises that came from the nun's clothing. Every movement created a swishing of material and a rattling of rosary beads. They entered the classroom. Her new classmates were sitting very straight, with their hands folded on their desks. Tamara thought their expressions were much too serious for children.

"This is Tamara. She is a new student. She has been attending public school, but her parents now realize she needs God's guidance. Everyone say, 'Welcome, Tamara'," the nun's no-nonsense voice announced.

"Welcome, Tamara," monotone voices responded.

"Very good, children. Now let's say our morning prayer."

Tamara froze. She had no idea what a morning prayer was. She looked at the children, searching for a friendly face to rescue her. They stood quietly. *I'll just copy what they do*, Tamara thought to herself. The children bowed their heads. Tamara bowed her head. The children put their hands together in front of their chests. She put her hands together. They began to pray. She began to mumble. The laughter of the children interrupted her concentration. *What are they laughing at?* she thought. She stole a glance at her new classmates. Her heart sunk. They were laughing at her.

Until that moment, Tamara had not noticed that Sister Margaret had turned and was facing the wall. Sister heard the laughter and glared at the children. They immediately stopped laughing.

With exaggerated gestures Sister placed her hands on Tamara's shoulders and turned her around. Tamara's eyes immediately spotted a large wooden crucifix. "Always face the cross when you pray," Sister announced in a loud voice, "not your classmates." Tamara could hear a few scattered snickers. She wondered if she would ever fit in.

There were over forty children in her class. The room was so crowded the desks touched. When it was time to leave for recess or lunch, one row of children exited and their desks were pushed over to make an aisle for the next row. Bathroom breaks were permitted only at recess and lunch because letting one student out was a major undertaking.

At least once a week a child would have an accident. Everyone would stare and giggle as the janitor pushed his mop under the cramped desks. The teasing at recess was merciless. Tamara swore she would not become a subject of such torment, but trying to coordinate her bodily functions with the school regiment often took incredible concentration. She would cross her legs, tap her foot, watch the clock and count the seconds so intently that she couldn't hear the lessons being taught.

Managing such a large class required strict discipline, but Sister Margaret never had a problem. Nuns instilled innate respect and fear in children. The rules were plentiful, and uniformity was uncompromisingly enforced.

When the children learned cursive handwriting, Tamara used her left hand. Sister immediately stopped her and announced to the class, "Left-handed people never have acceptable penmanship. Look at your desks. They are made for right-handed people. Left-handed people never fit in." Tamara thought such inflexibility was silly and unfair.

That night she complained to her father, but he made it clear he supported the school. "None of my children are going to be left-handed," he declared. "The world is designed for right-handed people. Left-handed people are freaks." So, Tamara struggled to be right handed and consistently received poor grades in penmanship.

Tamara adjusted to her new school and began to make friends. The fire changed everything. Her school didn't catch on fire, but an old Catholic school back East did. Kay heard it on the radio while she was ironing. She ran upstairs and turned on the television. She saw gruesome pictures of fire fighters carrying tiny bodies out of the flaming school building. Helpless mothers were sobbing, and angry bystanders were asking, "How could this happen?"

The newsman shook his head and said the old building should never have been allowed to house children. "It was in violation of every major fire code. Unfortunately, for these children, parochial schools are not subject to fire codes and inspections."

Kay jumped into the car and drove to school. She burst into the classroom and announced, "Tamara, come with me, right now! You aren't staying in this firetrap one more minute." And, just like that, Kay removed Tamara and her brother from the Catholic school. The next day she drove them to a public school.

"I don't want to change schools," protested Tamara.

"Well, I don't care what you want. My children aren't burning up in an old building," insisted Kay.

"But, I won't know anyone," cried Tamara. "They won't like me. They will laugh at me. I would rather burn up than change schools."

"Oh, stop being so dramatic," snapped Kay.

Tamara thought that was a strange comment coming from someone who took her children out of school in the middle of the day because a school across the country caught on fire. Once again, Tamara was introduced to a classroom of strangers.

"Everyone say, 'Good morning to Tamara.'"

"Good morning, Tamara," the voices unenthusiastically responded in unison.

"Very good, children. Now, everyone stand for the pledge of allegiance."

Tamara obediently bowed her head, turned towards the wall and brought her hands to her chest in a gesture of prayer. Laughter filled the classroom, and Tamara instinctually knew it was aimed at her. Her face began to burn, her hands began to tremble.

The teacher quieted the class, "Stop that children. It isn't nice to laugh at others." She whispered into Tamara's ear, "We don't pray here. We say the pledge of allegiance. Face the flag and put your right hand over your heart." As Tamara put her hands down and turned towards the flag, she could still hear random giggling. She hated being laughed at. She closed her eyes and thought, *I'm not going to like this school either.*

Tamara might have adjusted to that school, but the church agreed to let Tamara and her brother attend a newer parochial school, so they changed schools. A few years later when Tamara's little sister turned six, it became too expensive for her parents to have three children enrolled in private schools, so they went back to public school.

Tamara never fit in at school. She told herself it was because she moved around so much, but deep in her heart she knew it was because she was a round peg in a square hole.

She wanted to learn. She loved the challenge of trying to answer the teacher's questions. But, no matter how hard she tried, she could never get it right. Tamara was a visual, hands-on learner at a time when the only acceptable teaching technique was lecturing. She was a verbal processor in the days of quiet classrooms. Tamara was an attention-deficit child decades before anyone knew what a learning disability was. She was always in trouble for talking, squirming, interrupting, and daydreaming. It seemed to her that she spent the majority of her time standing in the corner, sitting in the hall, or waiting in the principal's office.

Friends

Tamara loved playing with other children. There were dozens of kids living on her block, and she wanted them to like her, but she was much too bossy.

In the summer, she would organize neighborhood musicals. She wrote the songs, designed the invitations, made the costumes, hung the lights, and cast the parts. She involved every child and some of the pets! The shows received standing ovations from impressed parents, but the triumph was always short-lived. By the time the curtain came down, Tamara had managed to alienate all the kids with her non-stop energy and dictatorial attitude. She never understood how their anger could outlast a successful production. Tamara knew she had a quick temper, but her outbursts were brief flashes of lightening. It seemed a silly waste of energy to hold a grudge and pout like so many of the other girls did.

Tamara's salvation was her passion for reading, which had been instilled in her by her grandmother's words. Tamara loved her grandmother with all her heart. Porky was the only adult who didn't seem annoyed by Tamara's endless questions and bottomless energy. She had long white hair that was swept into a bun and sparkling blue eyes that overflowed with warmth and playfulness. It seemed to Tamara that Porky possessed as much childish mischief as she did. Tamara's greatest sorrow was that Porky lived in Toronto and only visited once a year. Once, when Tamara was sitting on Porky's lap, wrapped in her safe arms, she confessed her deepest secret.

"The other kids are always mad at me. I don't fit in. I hate being different. I want to be like them."

Porky lifted Tamara's chin and wiped the tears from her eyes.

"You aren't different, Tamara. You are special. And, you will do special things. You must never want to be like everyone else," Porky's voice was soft and wise.

"But, I don't have any friends. I get lonely, and I hate being left out. They never invite me anywhere."

"You don't need friends, my dear." Porky's eyes twinkled and her whole being smiled as she continued, "You only need books. Books are magical. They will take you anywhere you want to go. They are your best friends. No one can ever take them away."

Kay

Tamara idolized her parents when she was young. She thought they were the most beautiful couple in the world. The neighborhood girls once voted her mother, Kay, and her father, Joe, the most handsome parents on the block. They were exciting people with active social lives. They threw wonderful, wild parties that were reported on the society page of the local newspaper.

Kay was the perfect hostess. She was funny and charming, and her life was an endless series of luncheons, style shows, and parties. Before marrying Joe, she had been a model and an artist, and she possessed a delightful sense of fashion and style. She was fanatical about staying thin. She never carried more than one hundred eighteen pounds on her five foot six inch frame. Kay ate a regular meal once a day. She allowed herself one piece of toast with her morning cup of tea. She regained her thin figure with remarkable speed after each of her five children was born. Kay said weight was a matter of self-respect and that men hated heavy women. She once told Tamara that Joe always threatened to leave her if she ever gained weight. He said fat women were disgusting because they exposed their lack of self-discipline to the world.

Tamara knew she was a disappointment to her mother. She did not have her mother's style and confidence. Tamara had poor vision, and she required glasses earlier than anyone in her school. Her mother bought her pointed, cat-eye frames covered with blue rhinestones. "They will accent the blue in your eyes, and then, no one will even notice that you are wearing glasses," Kay insisted. But, it was all for naught. Tamara's eyes could barely be seen through the coke-bottle thick lenses.

Then, she lost her front teeth. Tamara had the most perfectly straight teeth of all the children, until one summer day when she rode her brother's bike too fast down the street. She lost control, slid across the gravel, flew over the handlebars and snapped off her front teeth when her face impacted with the sidewalk. Tamara reached up and felt the large open space where her permanent teeth had been just seconds before. She sobbed and began digging wildly in the gravel.

Her mother ran out of the house and tried to pull Tamara up from the ground. Tamara pushed her mother's arm away screaming, "Leave me alone; I have to find them. We can glue them back on." But, they couldn't glue them back. In fact, they couldn't give her permanent caps for nearly a decade. Instead, there was a long succession of painful trips to the dentist and large, silver temporary caps that looked horrible and provided endless fodder for teasing.

One day while walking home from school, Tamara told a friend that she had a crush on Mark, the older boy who was walking in front of them. Her friend dared Tamara to whistle at him. Tamara accepted the dare. "Heh, Mark," she called out. To her chagrin, when she whistled, her silver cap flew out of her mouth and hit Mark in the face! She was mortified. (Like all embarrassing stories, this one took on a life of its own and followed her for years.)

Tamara did have one attractive asset. Her hair was thick, shiny and very long. It was the one thing about her appearance that she liked. Then, she started getting headaches. The family doctor checked her over and proclaimed, "It's her hair. It's much too heavy. Her headaches will stop if you cut it off."

Tamara was angry. She was convinced that her mother and father had put the doctor up to making the ridiculous demand. Her parents were always threatening to cut her hair if she didn't keep it in a ponytail and out of her eyes. The family barber snipped off the precious ponytail without the slightest appreciation for what he was taking from an insecure girl who had little else. To add insult to injury, her mother gave her a home perm. When the curlers came out, Tamara looked in the mirror and shrieked. It wasn't soft and curly like the picture on the box.

"It's awful!" yelled Tamara. "How could you make me look so awful?"

"It isn't awful," insisted her mother.

"It's wiry and frizzy. It looks like a poodle's butt. I won't go to school with a poodle butt on my head. Everyone will laugh at me."

"Stop that. No one will laugh at you."

"Yes, they will, they always do. I don't have any friends."

"Oh, nonsense. Everyone has friends."

"I don't. I don't know how to make friends," Tamara wailed in frustration.

"Oh, don't be silly. It is easy to make friends. You just have to be nice to the popular girls. Once they like you, everyone likes you," said Kay in a confident voice.

Tamara could see there was no point in going on. The horrible haircut and perm had sapped all her strength, and besides, she seldom agreed with her mother anymore. They lived in two different worlds. Kay was a lovely swan swimming with the other beautiful swans. Tamara was the ugly duckling struggling to keep afloat along the edge of the lake: ignored, dismissed, unacknowledged.

Joe

Joe was the hardest working person Tamara ever knew. He was a whirling dervish of energy, only different because each movement was deliberate and precise. He was extremely intelligent and could do three things at once. His intensity was both inspiring and draining to those around him. Joe demanded perfection from himself, his wife and five children. He inspected dishes for spots and floors for dust.

Joe's work often took him out of town. Tamara was grateful for those respites, because he was strict and short-tempered. He had no tolerance for Tamara's impulsive, strong personality, even though it was clear to others that she had inherited those attributes from him. Everyone said Tamara had her Italian father's quick temper and her Irish mother's quick tongue. She tried to please him but to no avail. She was constantly being reprimanded. And, to complicate things, Tamara never took her punishment without protest. She would loudly defend herself, which only made her father more furious and resulted in additional punishment.

Kay and Joe

Tamara loved her parents, but she hated the way they fought with each other. They would start by arguing over something trivial and then the battle of words would escalate into name-calling and threats. One of them would shout, "I don't care. I'm through arguing." And, the other would yell, "That's fine with me. Just don't say another word!" The children would hold their breath, hoping beyond hope, that this time the angry words would stop, but they never did. Kay and Joe were addicts, hooked on the adrenaline of confrontation.

The arguing always took an ugly turn when Joe and Kay had been partying. (Tamara did not understand until years later that alcohol was adding fuel to an already volatile relationship.) Tamara dreaded the nights when she would babysit her younger brothers and sister. She would stand at the window after midnight, with a knot in her stomach, praying that when her parents returned they would not slam the car doors. Slamming doors were storm warnings.

Ironically, the nights when the fights were the worst were the nights she felt closest to her sister, Vallia. Vallia had her father's thick, black hair and large brown eyes. Her father called Vallia his "black-eyed Susan." She was blessed with perfect vision, a lovely smile and a sweet nature that kept her out of trouble. Everyone adored her, except Tamara, who was very jealous of Vallia. But, all that was forgotten on the nights when their parents fought.

The two sisters shared a basement bedroom directly under their parents' bedroom. When angry words poured down from above, Vallia would bury her head in her pillow and sob. Tamara discovered the best way to alleviate Vallia's fear was to make her laugh, so when their parents room became a war zone, Tamara's room became a comedy club. If the fights became particularly fierce, Tamara would sneak upstairs to console her little brothers. Tamara believed it was her responsibility to rescue her siblings, because she was the strongest. She spent hours trying to figure out how to stop the fighting.

Once Tamara was watching her favorite television sit-com when the main couple had an argument. Television families in the fifties were immune to conflict, so Tamara was glued to the set wondering how this dilemma would be solved. At the end of the thirty-minute program, the children sang to their parents, and they all lived happily ever after. Tamara thought to herself, as she clicked off the TV set, *What a perfect idea. My parents love music. Why hadn't I thought of that before?*

She taught the song to her sister and brothers. The next time she was awakened by screams and yells, she gathered her siblings together outside their parents' bedroom door and led them in a harmonic rendition of:

> "You've got to give a little, take a little,
> And let your poor heart break a little.
> That's the glory of, that's the story of love."

Needless to say, the song did not create the reconciliation Tamara had seen on television.

When the battles escalated into slapping and hitting, Tamara and her older brother would march to their parents' room, pound on the door and scream for them to stop. Sometimes this strategy helped because it reminded Joe and Kay that there were children in the house. Other times it only resulted in Joe focusing his fury on the children, rather than Kay.

Tamara was never sure who she blamed most for the fights. It was clear that Kay had a poison tongue and knew exactly how to set Joe off. Tamara would listen to her mother start an argument with Joe and pray silently, *Please, Mother, stop. Please, shut up, and walk away.* Once the verbal battles became physical, Tamara transferred all fault to her father. But, in her heart, she blamed herself.

After all, she was the one who made everyone angry: her teachers, her parents, her brothers and sister, her friends. She was the one who was always in trouble. It only made sense that if things went wrong, they must be her fault.

A multi-faceted piece of glass was put into place.

The Lesson

Diversity

My strongest memories as a child all contain the messages, "You are difficult. You are different." In fairness to others, I was not an easy child. I was a moving turbo of energy. I was curious, verbal and hyperactive. I was impatient, stubborn and independent. In fairness to me, I wasn't given a chance.

I once overheard my grandfather telling a story of when I was a week old. Grampa was awakened by a loud pounding noise. He rushed to the attic bedroom and discovered my mother rocking my crib back and forth. Mother was oblivious to the fact that the crib was banging against the wall. I was screaming with the lungs of Pavarotti, and she was repeating in a mantra of frustration, "Make her stop . . . make her stop . . . make her stop." My grandfather swept me safely into his large arms and protested, "For God's sake, Kay, you could have hurt her."

My mother loved newborn babies. She loved to cuddle and dress them like dolls. But, once they became demanding toddlers, they overwhelmed her, especially when five active children came in close succession.

It was not my choice to be difficult or different. I was born with a strong personality. Unfortunately, I did not understand that we are all born with distinct personalities. God has made each of us unique and endowed us with special gifts. Some people are visionaries, while others are analytical. Some people are action-oriented leaders, while others are sensitive mainstays governed by the heart.

Scientists have debated "nature versus nurture" for years. Are we influenced more by our environment or by inheritance? It is clear that both play a role in making us who we are, but people with strong personalities are certainly born that way.

Differences can be seen in a hospital nursery when hungry infants are only hours old.

- One child waits patiently, observing all sounds and noises.
- One child curls into itself and whimpers softly.
- Another child squirms constantly and makes periodic, curt demands for assistance.
- Yet another disrupts the nursery with a cacophony of steady, ear-splitting wails.

And, anxious parents press their noses to the nursery window praying, "Oh please, don't let the screamer be mine!"

The greatest strength in a free country is the diversity of its citizens. Some people believe diversity should be minimized in order to make life more comfortable, but the cost of such comfort is much too high. We may gain temporary peace, but we eventually lose freedom itself. For if there was only one acceptable personality, which one would it be?

Chaos would certainly escalate if we eliminated the analysts who stay calm under pressure and solve problems. And perhaps the world would be less complicated without dreamers, but think how colorless and tedious it would be. Who would want to live in a world without the sensitive, stable people who give us roots and remind us that love is the essence of life? And, what a stagnant world it would be without trail-blazers who thrive on risk and accomplish what others only talk about.

It is clear that we are all inter-related. Our gifts build on the gifts of others. We are like sparkling lights on a Christmas tree. Each one different, each one glowing, and yet, each brighter when viewed as a whole.

Yes, diversity complicates our lives. It creates challenge and conflict, but it is the soul of independence, for without it, we are never truly free.

I recommend that every person take a personality test. There is a simple, yet effective personality test at the end of this book in Appendix A. I also recommend the book, Please Understand Me, by Keirsey and Bates. It goes without saying that people are complex and cannot be defined by one evaluation instrument, but discovering our own distinctive disposition helps us understand ourselves and appreciate others.

A personality test can reveal our strengths and pitfalls in communicating with others. Individuals are governed by their unique personalities, values, intellect and mental stability. Everyone reacts differently to life's challenges. It takes all types of people for a family, office, school or government to function and flourish. Therefore, we must spend more time accepting and appreciating each other and less time trying to change each other.

I spent most of my life trying to be someone else in order to "fit in." My energy level makes me a thousand-watt person in a hundred-watt world. I read books, attended workshops, observed others and tried to mirror the behavior of those who did "fit in." Of course, I was never successful, because, in the end, we cannot be someone else, we can only be ourselves. How I wish I had realized sooner that there is a place in the world for thousand-watt people. I would not have wasted so much valuable time and energy trying to be something I couldn't be. Instead, I would have focused on being the best "me" I could be.

I don't know what your gift is, but I know you have one. Perhaps you can sense pain in people and help them retrieve hope in their darkest moments. Perhaps you can mend a broken engine, make magic with clay or bring an instrument to life. Maybe you can construct a functional, yet, fanciful structure. Perhaps you can bring order to chaos or make computers perform at new levels, or you can rescue people from fear and lead them through the inevitable changes and challenges of life.

You must uncover your gift. Otherwise, you will spend your life tossed about on a sea of peer pressure trying to be someone you aren't. Even worse, you will go to your grave having never achieved your fullest potential, because you had no clear vision of whom God meant you to be.

The lessons I have learned, when I review my childhood vignettes, are clear:

- We are born unique and special.
- In order to fulfill our God-given potential, we must understand, acknowledge and accept our personality differences.

Chapter Three
Unanswerable Questions

The sun filtered through the trees in the alley, creating a paisley pattern of light that danced in harmony with the wind. Tamara's pudgy legs skipped quickly from one lighted spot to the next, as she invented her own game of dodge ball on nature's playground. Tamara was happy. She had been to a birthday party where she had eaten cake, watched a puppet show, and won at musical chairs. She held the pink plastic comb that was her prize and the envy of the other girls. Life was good for Tamara at that very moment.

She was disappointed when the foliage became denser and the light reflections disappeared. She was not ready to end the game. The thick bushes and trees reminded her that this was the part of the alley she did not like. It was too dark. The tree limbs hung like spider webs. The branches reached out like witch's fingers. She wanted to run, but she did not. Tamara played another game with herself, a game of bravery. She would not run. She would swallow her fear and walk steady and slow.

A branch snapped behind her. She turned and gasped. Someone was standing in the bushes.

"Don't be afraid, Tamara. You know me. I live down the street. That is a pretty white dress. Is it new?"

Tamara didn't want to talk to this man, but she had been told to answer adults when they spoke to her. She had also been told not to talk to strangers, but this man wasn't a stranger. He lived near her house. His gaze was too intense. Tamara turned her eyes away and hung her head.

"What are you holding, Tamara?"

She did not look up.

Tamara responded in a quiet voice, "It is my prize. I won it."

"Come here, I want to see your prize."

Tamara did not move.

"I am talking to you, Tamara. Come here, and show me what is in your hand," he said sternly.

Tamara recognized the tone of his voice. It was the tone her parents used when they spanked her for being stubborn. She took a deep breath, stepped closer to the bushes and opened her little fingers. He reached out, but his hand did not take the prize. It closed around her wrist.

"I won't hurt you. I want to see your new dress."

Tamara no longer cared about her game of bravery. She wanted to run. She pulled her arm, but he would not let go. She tried to cry out, but his hand went over her mouth.

"Don't yell, Tamara. If you yell, I will spank you very hard," he whispered gruffly.

He knelt down in front of her.

"This is a pretty dress, Tamara."

His hand touched her pink ribbon waistband, moved down the ruffle and under her dress. She tried to pull away. His face was very close to hers. His breath was sour.

"If you try to run away, I will catch you and hurt you."

He twisted her arm until she felt tears stinging her eyes.

"Don't cry!" he demanded.

His large hand squeezed tighter.

"That's a good girl, Tamara. You be a good girl, and I will make you feel real nice. You be a bad girl, and I will hurt you every time you go out to play."

He pushed her into the bushes and onto her back. The ground was hard. Tamara was more frightened than she had ever been in her short life. Her innocent mind did not grasp what was about to happen, but she knew this man was going to hurt her. She knew something was very wrong. He pulled down her pink lace panties.

Tamara closed her eyes as tightly as she could and cried softly.

"Mommy . . . Mommy . . . Oh, Mommy."

Fireworks began exploding in her head. She focused on the pretty fireworks—red, blue, white and yellow. She heard heavy breathing and a voice whispering.

"That's a good girl, Tamara. You are a good girl."

The fireworks grew louder. Then, the colors stopped exploding, and everything went black.

His voice sounded strange, as if muffled by cotton.

"Tamara, look at me. Open your eyes, and look at me."

When she opened her eyes, he was smiling.

"You were a good girl, Tamara. You made me happy. You must not tell anyone what happened. People would say you were a bad girl, and the police would come and take you away and put you in jail. I don't want you to go to jail. Do you want to go to jail?"

She was confused and frightened.

"No," she murmured.

"Good. What happened was your fault because you are so pretty and you wore that pretty dress, but I won't tell the police. Don't you tell anyone, or I will find you."

His threat planted unimaginable fear in Tamara's vulnerable heart. She closed her eyes and laid very still. She heard him walk away. She did not move for a very long time.

Tamara sat up slowly. She looked at her skirt and gasped. Her new dress was dirty and the ruffle torn. Her mind was racing with questions, *What did he do to me? Why did he hurt me?* Hampered by the limited reasoning ability of a child, she tried to make sense of what had happened.

He said I was pretty. He said I was a good girl. But, he hurt me, so I must have done something wrong. She felt pain in a place that had never hurt before. *There must be something wrong with that place. That place must be bad. I must be bad.*

The irrational ideas rushed through her impressionable mind and left their imprint– like a computer. When the disk was full, she pushed the off button and stored the data.

Tamara's little fingers roamed over the torn ruffle and crinkled skirt. She tried to smooth out the wrinkles. *I tore my dress. It is my fault. I am a bad girl.* Something in her mind started to object, but as she pushed at her dress, she pushed those objections away. *I fell down and tore my dress. I am bad.* Harder and harder she pushed the dress, and harder and harder she pushed the horrifying memories into the deep recesses of her mind.

She stood up and walked home. She went in the back door, changed her clothes and put her dress in the hamper. Later her mother found the dirty, torn dress, and demanded an explanation. Tamara looked at the floor.

"I ran down the alley. I tore my dress. I am a bad girl."

She got a spanking.

And a muted piece of glass was added to the window.

The Lesson

Be Gentle with Yourself

I recently heard a man say that children who are violently abused can never be normal. There have been times in my life when I would have agreed with this man, but now I know he is wrong. What happened to me was a tragedy, but it did not prevent me from living a healthy, happy, normal life. It did leave scars.

Being assaulted as a child is much like being burned. There are places that stop hurting almost immediately because the skin dies. There are other wounds that hurt for a long time because they are slowly repairing themselves. Eventually, the burn heals, the pain ceases and the scar fades. The wounded place, however, remains sensitive and vulnerable.

When I was a child, I trusted that the world was safe and adults wouldn't hurt me. But an adult did hurt me. No one heard my cries. No one rescued me. In one awful moment, my innocence was shattered, and I experienced the fear of being powerless. Suddenly, I found myself asking the kinds of questions that other children didn't ask because they were too busy being children. I asked myself the kinds of questions that couldn't be answered without acknowledging the darkest side of life.

Children develop ways to survive when they discover they are at the mercy of those who choose to inflict pain. Part of that survival process is to redefine reality in light of the trauma. When I realized that I couldn't make sense out of the senseless, I created a new truth that would explain what happened.

I decided that people couldn't be trusted and that I should expect bad things to happen. That outlook was indeed cynical for a child, but it actually provided me with peace. Pain didn't seem so scary once I accepted that it was always going to be part of my life. By taking the surprise out of misfortune, I made it tolerable.

I survived by burying the trauma deep in my subconscious, until a later time when I would be old enough to answer the questions that no child should have to ask.

There is a great deal of debate about recovered memories. I choose not to discuss the conflicting opinions of experts. I cannot speak for others, but I can speak about what I know to be fact from my own experience. I know the mind is capable of burying pain until a person is capable of processing that pain.

Ask any group of women about childbirth. They will recall vivid memories of the smells, sights and sounds. They will say that labor hurt, but they will not be able to describe the exact pain. Many will say if they remembered the pain, they would not have had more children.

Ask a group of people about the pain of losing loved ones. They will recall being emotionally and physically numb through the first days as they dealt with the initial shock of loss. Many will say if they weren't desensitized, they would have died from the anguish.

What happened to me should not happen to any child, but, unfortunately, it has happened to other boys and girls. It took hard work with professional counselors for me to acknowledge and accept the scars that were produced.

Finding a positive lesson in this situation was one of the most difficult challenges in writing this book. I resisted for a long time because I did not want to imply that what happened was acceptable. But, prayer and time helped me to realize that finding a survival message in a trauma does not make that trauma a positive experience. It only means we are willing to grow.

As I view this tragedy through the eyes of an adult, I do see a very valuable lesson:

- When bad things happen, our bodies, minds and souls will activate powerful survival mechanisms that make it possible for us to heal and recover.

If you are struggling with crisis or pain, it will help to remember the following:

Give yourself permission to be numb.
It is a defensive mechanism.

Give yourself permission to hurt.
It is a part of the process.

Give yourself permission to talk.
It allows those who love you to be a part of your healing.

Give yourself permission to be angry with God.
It shows that you trust Him.

Give yourself permission to lean on God.
It shows that you know Him.

Most of all, be gentle with yourself.

You will survive.

Chapter Four
Abandoned

Tamara was terrified. Early that morning her mother had packed the car with Tamara's belongings, and they left Montana. They were driving to Canada where Tamara would attend FCJ, a Catholic convent for girls.

Tamara had cried most of the night. She was ashamed of herself, for she knew at thirteen years old she should be beyond crying. She still remembered two months ago when her mother had yelled, "We aren't going to put up with your antics anymore. You are going to boarding school young lady. Maybe a year in a convent will change your attitude." At the time, Tamara had thought it was another one of her mother's hollow threats, but it wasn't, for here she was, driving towards a place she knew nothing about.

"Please, Mother," she pleaded, "I will try harder in school. I'll get better grades."

"It isn't just your grades, Tamara. You argue about everything."

"I won't argue anymore."

"It's not the just the arguing. I don't have the energy for your father and you kids . . .."

"Then, why don't you send them away? Why am I the one?"

"Because, you are the one who wears me out: your questions—your crying—your temper tantrums—everything is a crisis with you. Don't you understand?"

"No, I don't, " responded Tamara. "I don't understand anything . . .."

"Welcome to the club," snapped her mother.

"Please, I will be good. Don't send me away."

Her mother said nothing.

Tamara knew her great aunt had attended FCJ sixty years before, but that knowledge did not prepare her for the aging building. It was immense, square and wooden. As they entered, it become obvious the inside was also void of character. It was stark. It was dark. Tamara felt a chill down her spine. As it turned out, her fear was justified.

A six-foot nun with a grotesque, bulbous nose and cold eyes approached. "You must be Tamara. You are just in time for evening mass. Say good-bye to your mother, and come with me."

"Please, Mother, I can change," Tamara tried one last time.

"No, you can't. Good-bye."

And so began the eighth grade for Tamara. The girls at the school ranged in age from six to eighteen. Tamara wondered what terrible crime a six-year-old could have committed to warrant such banishment. She later learned most of the girls were from wealthy families. Professional and social commitments kept their parents much too busy to raise children.

The rigidity of life within the boarding school was unfathomable. The plaque in the hallway explained that FCJ stood for Faithful Christ Jesus, but the girls said it stood for First Class Jail.

All the girls slept in an enormous dorm divided into cubicles. Each cubicle was separated by curtains, like a hospital room. There was just enough room in each space for a bed and small bed table. A basin sat uniformly on each table.

A clanging bell woke them at precisely five forty-five a.m. They stood in line at the one bathroom sink to fill their basins, then returned to their cubicles for sponge baths. Once a week they were assigned fifteen minutes in the evening or morning for a tub bath. It was so cold in the morning that water left in the basin overnight would freeze. Whenever the younger girls were assigned a morning bath, they willingly gave their weekly tub time to the older girls, who were thrilled to bathe twice a week.

Every morning after they washed, the girls stripped their beds, shook out their blankets and hung them over the cubicle railings. At precisely six thirty a.m., they were escorted, in a perfect line, to the chapel where they were required to attend confession. Ironically, it was very difficult to sin in this place. When they weren't in church, they were in class. They never left the convent grounds, and they were surrounded by nuns. Nonetheless, they were required to search their consciences everyday for sins to confess. It became impossible to tell the difference between normal, prepubescent behavior and serious transgressions. Everything became distorted. Soon after arriving at FCJ, they began to feel guilty about every deed, every comment, every thought.

They were required to kneel the entire mass on un-sanded, un-padded pews. The younger children would rest their bottoms against the pew in order to give their knees a respite.

The nuns would swat them with a stick. The girls were grateful for those times when they could stand and sing.

After church they returned to the dorm, made their beds, attended breakfast, and went to class. They broke for lunch, and immediately after eating, returned to their classrooms for the rosary. This was the most torturous part of the day because they were required to kneel on cement floors.

Tamara would burrow her eyes into the clock, willing it to go faster. In the beginning, the girls would try to subtly speed up the recitation but their efforts never shortened the twenty-six minute rosary time. Tamara soon learned to smuggle an extra pair of socks into the pocket of her uniform. She would wait until the pain was unbearable and then slide the socks under her knees. Tamara thought it was silly to pray under such circumstances. She could think of nothing but the pain in her hips, legs and knees. No matter how hard she tried to be devout, within minutes she was praying, "Please, God, let this end."

At three thirty p.m., they were allowed a thirty minute break in the yard. The only authorized entertainment was hopscotch. At first, Tamara found it pathetic that teenagers could enjoy a child's game, but she soon became as competitive as the rest of the girls. Then, it was study hall, dinner, dishes, more study hall, formal prayers in the chapel and bed. It was tedious, but tolerable, until the lights were out.

That was when the loneliness enveloped her. Tamara missed her little brothers. She missed Shane's large brown eyes and slapstick antics. He always had a knack for making her laugh. She especially missed Pat. When she closed her eyes she could recall the pure wonder and joy she had felt when her mother brought Pat home from the hospital. He was a perfect, trusting little creature, and she had vowed the minute she laid eyes on him to be his keeper. Protecting him from the craziness at home had been her mission. She worried about him constantly.

Tamara was surprised to discover how much she missed her sister, Vallia. She had always been jealous of Vallia. Like all sisters, they argued over clothes and toys. But, they always talked about the events of the day before falling off to sleep. She ached to say good-night to Vallia.

Tamara wrote daily letters to her parents. She tried every strategy to persuade them to bring her home. She confessed that she had been a bad child and promised she would no longer be moody or rebellious. She thanked them for this great opportunity to grow. She espoused mature thoughts about the meaning of life and her new devotion to God. She pleaded! They ignored all her letters.

The most unbearable letters were the ones she received from friends. They wrote about boys, music, and parties. She hid the letters under her pillow and cried because life was passing her by.

Tamara began to sink deeper and deeper into depression. She began to daydream so often that she could not tell the difference between the bland life around her and the murky fantasies in her head. Then, she began to get ill. It started with a rash on her arms. She scratched her arms until they were bleeding and scabby. Her eyelids developed styes. A hang nail became so infected, she could not hold a pencil. Her entire hand throbbed. She could not sleep. Finally, Mother Superior directed that she be taken to the doctor. When the doctor took the bandage off her hand, he expressed concern.

"This child has gangrene. She could lose her finger. How could you let it go this far?"

"She kept it covered," responded the nun.

"What about her eyes? She couldn't cover those infections."

"She won't eat properly," explained the nun defensively.

"This child is run down, and I suspect she is suffering from depression."

"I don't think so, Doctor. She is just moody and disagreeable."

"Well, I want you to contact her parents, and tell them your school doesn't agree with her," directed the doctor.

Tamara couldn't believe it. The doctor had said that boarding school wasn't good for her. He was telling the nuns to contact her parents. She was so happy that she didn't feel the doctor lance and drain her finger. Finally, she was going home.

She didn't go home. Instead, she received a letter from her parents saying they were very disappointed with her rebellious attitude. They complained of paying for the extra medical treatment and vitamins. As a punishment, they had decided that she would not be allowed to come home during the next school break.

Tamara crunched the letter into a small ball and crawled into bed. She felt herself falling into a deep abyss. The dark colors swirled through her head and then moved through her body until the painful throbbing permeated every fiber of her being. She knew the pain would not stop until she was free from this place. She closed her eyes and designed plans for escape. Intricate plans. Extraordinary plans that filled her with hope. But, when she opened her eyes, she realized none of the plans would work. The only escape was to sleep.

"If I could sleep forever, it would numb the pain," she told herself. "Nothing would ever hurt again." It was then that Tamara devised her plan for survival. "If two aspirin can numb the pain in my hand, dozens would numb the pain in my heart," she rationalized.

Each girl was allowed to keep two aspirin in the drawer of her bed stand. Tamara began borrowing their aspirin. Her excuses were creative.

"Please, can I borrow your aspirin. I dropped mine in the sink." "I gave mine away and now I have a headache." "I used mine this morning."

Slowly, methodically, she collected aspirins in an envelope under her mattress. The plan gave her new energy.

A Treasure

Everything changed a week later when she received a letter from home that contained exciting news. One of her mother's friends had a daughter who skated with the Canadian Ice Capades. The Ice Capades were coming to Edmonton, and the skater had agreed to take Tamara out for lunch.

For the first time in months Tamara had something to look forward to. She circled the day on her calendar with a red crayon. She traded three future bath times in order to bathe and wash her hair that morning. Tamara put on a clean uniform and arrived in the school's foyer one hour early. The young skater was right on time. She had bright eyes and red lipstick. She was so animated that her energy filled the taxi. Tamara could not take her eyes off the graceful hands. Her long fingers punctuated every statement.

At lunch the skater told exciting stories of performing throughout the country for large, appreciative audiences. It was the most glamorous life Tamara had ever heard of.

"Oh my goodness," exclaimed the young skater, "I have been babbling on and on about myself, and I haven't asked you one question. Tell me about your life."

For the first time in her thirteen years, Tamara could think of nothing to say. The silence became unbearable.

"The truth is, I have no life," Tamara explained.

"Of course, you do, you are a teenager. Tell me about your friends–your favorite music–what do you do for fun?"

Tamara closed her eyes and tried to envision her life. All she could see were the dark colors of the convent.

"I have no friends," she murmured, "I have no music. I have nothing."

Tamara dropped her head and felt tears welling in her blue eyes. She glared at the golden border of the china plate and willed herself not to cry, but the tears would not obey. They came slowly at first, and then faster until they dropped off her chin and onto her food. She covered her mouth with the linen napkin. Her soft whimper became muffled sobs. Months of despair and loneliness would not be denied.

The skater was frightened. After all, she was just a young woman herself. As she watched Tamara's small shoulders shake with sorrow, the skater realized that in her twenty years she had never experienced such despair. "Tell me about life at the convent," she whispered.

In a halting voice, Tamara began to tell her stories. She never lifted her head, and the tears never stopped. She told of the monotony, the rigidity, and the loneliness. She told of the cold dorm room where water froze in her basin and the rationed baths. She told of the silly hopscotch, the endless studying, and the torturous rosaries.

"And, the worst part is confession. I search my soul every morning to find exactly what I have done wrong. I tell the priest, and I am truly sorry for being sad and mad and bad. But, the next day I must do it again. The guilt never ends."

Finally, she lifted her head with adult resolve.

"I don't want to live. All I want to do is sleep, sleep forever."

The skater wiped tears from her own eyes.

"This isn't right. I'm going to call your mother tonight and tell her how awful FCJ is. I'm going to tell her how sad you are. I will help you get out of there."

"Thank you," said a smiling Tamara.

Her smile, however, was motivated by courtesy, not hope. She had learned that no one could help her, not the wise old doctor and certainly not this sweet, young woman.

They sat in silence and then the face of the beautiful skater brightened.

"I have an idea. I won't take you back right away. Let's go to the skating rink. You can meet my friends and watch us practice. Will you get in trouble if you get back late?"

"Oh, no, it will be fine," Tamara declared with great confidence.

Her confidence was genuine because she knew of no punishment that could possibly outweigh the pleasure of going to the Ice Capades' practice.

Tamara sat in the grandstands waiting for practice to begin. She felt like the most important person in all the world. The skaters came out of the dressing room and waved at her. Music trumpeted over the loud speakers, and the skaters whirled on the ice, as if on air. She clapped, cheered and whistled. Surely, no audience could have been more appreciative. When the practice ended, they gave her an autographed poster. Tamara was so overwhelmed with gratitude, she could hardly find her voice. "Oh thank you," she breathed, "it is a treasure, and I will keep it forever."

When it was time to say good-bye she hugged the young skater for as long as she dared. She wanted to transfer warmth and love to this special woman who had entered her life for one brief afternoon and rekindled hope and happiness.

On her way back to FCJ, Tamara closed her eyes in the taxi and held the poster. As she ran her hand over the raised letters, she could see the skaters soaring through the air, free of restraint and fear. Upon her return to the convent, she hid the poster in the back of her old wooden locker. She promised herself she would hold it every day and remember the beautiful men and women who relished life.

Tamara ran off to dinner and recounted her afternoon adventure for everyone at her table. The younger girls were mesmerized. The older girls were skeptical.

"You are making that up," charged one of the oldest girls who usually ignored her.

"I am not," Tamara insisted. "I went to the Ice Capades, and I watched practice, and all the skaters gave me a poster."

"We don't believe you."

"I can prove it. I have the poster hidden in my locker. I'll show it to you after chores."

Tamara washed dishes as quickly as possible. She couldn't wait to impress the older girls with her treasure.

"Maybe this will make them like me," she thought. "Maybe I won't be so alone."

The girls were waiting when she entered the room. She opened the small locker and reached behind her coat and books. She couldn't feel the poster! Her heart sank.

"It isn't here." The younger girls looked disappointed. The older girls started to laugh.

"We knew you made it up."

"No I didn't," she insisted.

"It was here. I went to the Ice Capades and they signed it just for me. One of you stole it, and I am going to report you to Mother Superior."

Tamara threw back her shoulders and marched from the room. Anger gave her the courage to knock on Mother Superior's door.

"Come in," came the authoritative voice.

Tamara opened the door.

"I am sorry to bother you, Mother Superior, but someone stole something from me."

"That is a very serious accusation. Our girls do not steal."

"But, someone did, and it was very valuable," Tamara countered.

"I don't see how that could be possible. No student is allowed to have valuables at the convent. Worldly possessions distract from our spiritual focus."

"But, it was a gift. It was a poster from the Ice Capades and . . .."

"Oh, yes, I heard about that. It was reported to Sister Mary that you were bragging about a silly souvenir, so, she threw it out."

"No!" yelled Tamara. "You couldn't have. You had no right."

"Don't raise your voice to me, young lady. Of course, we had the right. You know the rules. You cannot possess anything that the other girls do not have. You must not bring attention to yourself. That is why you all dress the same and wear your hair the same. Worldly possessions cause segregation and pride."

"But, it was a treasure . . .," pleaded Tamara.

"Nonsense, the only treasures are those given by God."

"And, how do you know God didn't give it to me?" snapped Tamara.

Mother Superior's response was strong.

"You report to chapel immediately, and say two rosaries. One for your blasphemy and one for falsely accusing your fellow students of stealing. You are dismissed."

Tamara knelt alone in the chapel. Her fingers moved systematically over the rosary beads. There was no peace in her penance. The monotonous routine had long ago become a punishment rather than a prayer. Her mind began to wander. She glanced around the chapel, her eyes stopping on the confessional.

At least tomorrow I will have something to confess, she thought.

And then she began to focus on her sins. Soon the anger she felt when leaving Mother Superior's office was replaced by guilt.

"I was wrong for wanting the poster," she sighed. "I was wrong for showing off. I was wrong for thinking I was special."

Once again pain and despair consumed her. *I was bad. I was always bad.*

By the time Tamara had returned to the dorm, she knew what she must do. She filled her glass with water and closed the curtain around her cubicle. She took the envelope from under the mattress and began to swallow the accumulated aspirins. Tamara was so intent on her task that she didn't hear the small child pull back the cubicle curtain.

"Tamara, what are you doing with all those pills?" questioned the wide-eyed six-year-old.

She ignored the child's question.

"What are you doing here?"

"I came to thank you for telling me about the skaters and the poster. It must have been wonderful. I am so glad you shared your story with us."

"Maybe I just made it up," grumbled Tamara sarcastically.

"Oh, you didn't make it up. No one could make up such a grand adventure."

"Thank you! Now, you better get in bed before they turn the lights out."

"Okay."

The little girl turned to leave and then hesitated.

"Why were you taking so many pills?" she asked.

"Because, I hurt."

"Where do you hurt?"

"Everywhere."

"Is it okay to take so many pills?"

Tamara looked at the child's trusting eyes.

"No, it isn't okay, but it will be our secret. You must not tell anyone."

Late in the night, the small child found the burden of secrecy too heavy to carry. She woke the dorm leader and told her what Tamara had done.

The Hospital

Someone was shaking Tamara. Shaking her hard, but she couldn't wake up. She didn't want to wake up. She heard voices, but they were far away in another place, another time. A light was shining in her eyes. It hurt. "Call the ambulance." The voice sounded like Mother Superior's, but the voice sounded anxious, and Tamara knew nothing could make Mother Superior anxious.

More bright lights. And, noise, so much noise. "Tamara, I am the doctor. We must pump your stomach. I am going to put a tube down your throat. This will not be pleasant. You must swallow." It hurt. She tried to call out *stop*, but her voice didn't work. She tried to push them away, but her arms didn't work. She drifted back to sleep, but it was no longer a peaceful sleep.

"How are we feeling today?" asked the nurse. Tamara started to respond, but stopped. Her throat burned. "Your throat will be sore for awhile. It's to be expected. They put a tube into your stomach. I will be back this afternoon to take you for a walk as the doctor prescribed." The nurse disappeared with the same swift efficiency that had carried her into the room.

Tamara stared out the window. She could not see details because she wasn't wearing her glasses, but she could tell the sun was bright. *A perfect day for hopscotch*, she thought sarcastically and memories of the convent filled her head. A loud, involuntary moan escaped from her lips.

"Are you okay? Should I call the nurse?," asked a gentle voice.

Tamara turned her head towards the voice and saw an elderly lady sitting on the bed next to hers.

"Oh, Gramma Porky! It's you! I am so glad you are here," Tamara exclaimed. "I have been so lonely and scared."

"My name is Elizabeth," said the smiling lady. "I am not Porky, but I am a grandma. I have a dozen grandchildren, and one more wouldn't be a problem, so I can be yours, too, if you would like."

"Thank you," responded Tamara. "That would be nice."

"They brought you in early this morning. The nurse said you took pills. How could one so young have so much to escape from?"

Before Tamara could respond, the door opened and Mother Superior entered with two other nuns. She announced her presence with a loud voice seething with anger.

"Well, I hope you are proud of yourself. What you have done is against the law, you know. A judge could send you away. We have called your parents and told them you are no longer welcome at FCJ."

Tamara was too frightened to respond.

"Excuse me," interrupted Elizabeth, "but, the nurse said that Tamara wasn't to talk. In fact, I clearly heard the doctor say she was to have no visitors for twenty-four hours. I think I had better push this button and get the nurse in here right away."

"That won't be necessary," snapped Mother Superior. "We were just leaving."

As soon as the door closed behind the nuns, Tamara's face broke into a smile.

"Oh, thank you," she whispered hoarsely.

"Well one thing is for certain, that scary lady would make me take pills," Elizabeth said as she smiled.

Tamara giggled out loud. Elizabeth pulled her chair to Tamara's bed.

"Now, I will sit very close so you don't have to strain your voice. Tell me everything."

Tamara found Elizabeth easy to talk to because she expressed no judgement. She rubbed Tamara's arm and responded with sincere concern.

"Oh, that sounds so painful . . . who would do such a thing . . . you must have been so mad . . ."

Time passed quickly, and they were both surprised when the nurse returned.

"It's time for you to walk," the nurse announced.

"I will take her," said Elizabeth, "I could use the exercise too."

"Good," uttered the nurse, "I really am quite busy."

Tamara was surprised by the weakness in her legs.

"Just take your time, dear," assured Elizabeth. "I'm no speed demon myself."

They giggled. Tamara was oblivious to the sterile surroundings. She felt herself relaxing, trusting. They were returning to the room when Tamara froze, her eyes filling with fear.

"What's wrong?" asked Elizabeth.

"It's my mother. She is over there, talking to the nurse. How did she get here so fast? I am going to be in so much trouble."

"No, Tamara, you won't be in trouble. She will be so glad you are okay."

Tamara dropped Elizabeth's arm and darted into the room. She looked around for somewhere to hide. She jumped into the closet and closed the door behind herself.

"What a strange thing to do," Elizabeth murmured.

An attractive woman approached Elizabeth. "Excuse me, but have you seen my daughter? The nurse said this is her room."

Elizabeth raised her hand and hesitantly pointed to the closet. "She is in there."

Kay opened the closet door and saw her child squatted in the corner.

"Tamara, what in the name of God are you doing in there. Get up!" Kay yelled. "Do you know what you have done? I have friends in this town. Friends who work at this hospital. Do you know how embarrassed I am. What are they going to think? What are they going to say?"

Elizabeth was stunned. She stepped in front of Kay.

"Stop that right now! This child has been through a great deal and it serves no purpose for you to yell at her."

"Excuse me, but who are you?" grilled Kay.

"I am her friend," said Elizabeth confidently.

"Well, I am her mother, and if I . . ."

Elizabeth cut off Kay's words.

"Do you love your daughter?"

"Of course, I love her!"

"You aren't showing it very well."

"You have no idea what this child has put me through," Kay rebutted. "Her father and I flew here as soon as we could. We have been worried sick . . ."

Elizabeth interrupted Kay's tirade, "I suggest you stop yelling and tell her that."

Kay shook her head.

"Right now, she doesn't deserve love."

"None of us deserve it. We just need it."

"This isn't the time or the place," objected Kay.

Elizabeth placed her hand on Kay's arm.

"There isn't a better time or place. Years ago, I had an argument with my oldest daughter. She left in a huff. I wanted to run after her, but my pride stopped me. She was in an accident. When I got to the hospital, it was too late to tell her. You are a very lucky lady."

And with that, Elizabeth left the room.

Revelation

The hospital released Tamara the next day. The doctor said she had not really intended to kill herself. It was just a cry for attention, he explained. If it had been a real suicide attempt she would not have told one of the girls about her plans. Mother Superior made arrangements for Tamara's previous school in Montana to administer her final exams. If she passed, she would be promoted to ninth grade.

Her father did not come to the hospital. He had business to attend to. Tamara was worried that he would yell at her when she arrived at the airport for the flight home. But, he did not yell. In fact, he smiled warmly and helped her up the stairs. Once they were seated, Kay made Tamara promise to never tell anyone what she had done.

"We will say you came home from school a month early because you got ill. You were hospitalized with an appendix attack," insisted Kay.

"But, I had my appendix out last summer," Tamara declared.

"Quit arguing with me and do what I say. Do you want people to think you are crazy? That's what they'll say you know. They will say you are crazy."

"Shut up, Kay," Joe snapped. "Leave the girl alone. Who cares what people say?"

It was the only time Tamara could remember her father coming to her defense. She never forgot that for one brief moment her father had acknowledged and accepted her.

No one spoke on the flight home. The silence between her parents was laden with tension, but Tamara didn't care. The quiet gave her time to reflect on the past few days. In her heart Tamara knew the doctor was right. She had not wanted to die. She had just wanted to escape. As she gazed out the window of the plane she found it impossible to recall the despair that had caused her to take such desperate action. Yesterday the pain had been unbearable, but today it seemed insignificant.

At that moment, the plane broke through the cotton candy clouds. Bright sunshine splashed through the window and warmed her face. Tamara thanked God that she was alive. She promised herself and God that she would always remember:

- The joy of being alive surpasses the deepest pain of depression.

And, a heavy piece of the window was put into place.

The Lesson

Breaking Free of Depression

Depression is one of the most debilitating of all illnesses. It is like childbirth. It cannot be understood by those who have not experienced it. People can sympathize, but they cannot truly empathize until they have been trapped in a gloom that encases the soul in cement.

It can strike anyone at anytime. Even the strong find themselves in the incapacitating, murky, black place called depression. No one is immune to depression, not the CEO of a Fortune 500 company, not the homeless Viet Nam veteran, and not the award-winning teacher. It sends the most positive person careening down a cavern of darkness. It traps the most successful person in a pit of self doubt. It infects the most loved person with self loathing. It strips the most productive person of all desire to produce.

Depression may be situational: linked to a life crisis such as the death of a loved one or a divorce. A restrictive job or relationship can cause depression. FCJ was a stifling place where I could not express my creativity and spontaneity, the attributes that are such a strong part of who I am.

Depression may be clinical: linked to an unexplainable chemical imbalance. Only medical help can offer relief from such depression.

And depression may have no cause—it just arrives like a thief, stealing mental stability and personal peace.

FCJ was not the first or last time I wrestled with depression. It is the most vivid because I received the false and dangerous messages: people who experience depression are bad, depression should be ignored and others are threatened when our pain intrudes into their territory. These false messages thwarted my personal growth for many years by increasing the power depression had over me. As an adult, I was able, with the help of professionals, to erase those false messages and replace them with valuable lessons.

It is true that the passage of time often relieves depression, especially if it is caused by a specific crisis. A depressed person, however, must not sit and wait for things to improve. Action must be taken. It is important to seek help from counselors. Traditional medicine is necessary in many cases, and alternative medicine can be helpful. We must address depression before it becomes a cancer, consuming and ravaging every aspect of our lives.

People cannot conquer depression alone. Ironically, depression tricks people into believing no one cares and no one can be trusted. That trickery is one of the cruelest aspects of depression. A depressed person is harmed, not helped by isolation. We must, of course, be cautious with our trust, but we must confide our fears and anguish to someone. And, if our first attempts to reach out are met with rejection and apathy, we must force ourselves to reach out again and again until we find someone who cares.

Our society has become accepting of physical illness, but, unfortunately, there are still people who are frightened by mental illness. That intolerance comes from fear. People do not want to acknowledge that serious depression could strike them. Therefore, those of us who have walked through the dark caverns of depression must acknowledge the walk. In doing so, we will help those who are still lost in the caverns realize they are not alone and there is a passage out.

One of the best lessons I learned at the convent is that the despair of yesterday will dim in tomorrow's light. The darkness of depression is not eternal.

Depression may shroud the brightest pieces of glass in our windows with heavy shadows, but it does not permanently discolor the glass.

In later years, when I struggled with disappointment, helplessness, and guilt, I would remind myself of the lessons I learned from FCJ:

- Overcoming depression requires action.
- Seek professional help from counselors and doctors.
- Accept support from friends and family.
- Move forward, one minute at a time, one day at a time.
- Depression will pass.
- The joy of being alive surpasses the deepest pain of depression.

Chapter Five
Finding Strength

Tamara heard the girls' laughter echoing down the hallway. She jumped up from the floor and wiped the tears from her face. She rubbed the words, *DON'T CARE* off the window. She grabbed a book from her suitcase, opened it and plopped down on the bed. By the time the girls entered the dorm room, there was no sign of the vulnerable, lonely teenager who had been crying just seconds before.

Priory

"Welcome to Priory."

Tamara looked up from her book and saw an angelic face.

"I am Sarah. I see you like to read. So do I. We are going to be great friends. I am so sorry that you got here too late for evening prayers."

Oh no, thought Tamara. *I have a goody-two-shoes for a roommate. My luck!*

"Don't worry, Sarah is the only one who likes to pray," one of the other girls groaned.

"That isn't true," protested Sarah. "The nuns like to pray. I'm going to be a nun," she said to Tamara.

"Yeah, right," snickered Tamara, "unless you meet Mr. Right."

The girls laughed. Sarah cringed. Introductions were made, and Tamara convinced her roommates to take her on a quick tour.

Priory was such an improvement over FCJ that it seemed almost luxurious. There were two large bathrooms with enough sinks for everyone and showers plentiful enough that everyone could shower daily. The dining room was spacious and the recreation room even had a television, although viewing privileges were restricted to weekends. There was a small break room on the dorm floor that had candy and pop machines.

The most impressive room was the chapel. It was designed to resemble a stonecutter's cave. It had a high, curved ceiling and rounded stone walls that provided perfect acoustics for the immense pipe organ that stretched the entire width of the altar. Small intricate stained glass windows speckled the walls.

"Wait until you see the windows in the daylight. The sun shines right through . . ." Sarah said to Tamara.

"And sends rainbows dancing across the pews," Tamara interjected in a voice so soft no one could hear.

"Isn't it just lovely?" asked Sarah, her voice airy with awe.

"I think it's heaven," responded Tamara loudly.

"You do?" smiled Sarah.

"Sure," snickered Tamara. "It has padded kneelers. You can't get much closer to heaven than that."

The girls laughed.

"It is my favorite place in the world," Sarah protested.

"Let's get out of here," insisted Tamara. "This place makes me feel so guilty; it'll take two priests to hear my confession."

They headed for the door. Tamara deliberately lagged behind. After the others left, she took one last glimpse of the majestic chapel. She knew this was going to be her favorite place too, but she promised herself she would never let anyone else know.

The girls were talking excitedly when they entered the dorm room. Sister Ruth was waiting for them with a stern look on her face.

"Where have you been? You are late. Lights should have been out ten minutes ago."

Everyone hung there heads, except Tamara who stepped boldly forward.

"It was my fault. I wanted to see this place," she announced.

"You should have waited until tomorrow," interrupted Sister Ruth.

"But, what if I died during the night?" Tamara said with a solemn look on her face.

"Why would you say such a strange thing?" asked Sister Ruth.

"Well, you see, Sister," Tamara explained in a quiet voice, "every night when I was a child, my parents would say that prayer all parents say to children. You know the one, 'Now I lay me down to sleep, I pray the Lord my soul to keep. If I should die before I wake. I pray the Lord my soul to take.' I know my parents meant well but that prayer scared me to death. Imagine going to bed every night thinking you were going to die in your sleep. I decided right then never to go to bed leaving something important undone."

Sister Ruth could not tell if Tamara was serious or putting on an act for the other girls. She studied Tamara's face but could detect no insincerity. She decided to give her the benefit of the doubt.

"Well I can see you meant no harm, but we follow a strict schedule at Priory, including lights out at nine, and I advise you to follow the rules. Now get ready for bed, quickly and quietly."

The nun stood in the door, with her back to the room, while the girls changed into their pajamas. She waited in the bathroom while they brushed their teeth and used the toilet. She led them back to the room, waited until they were in bed, and turned out the lights. As soon as she left the room, Sarah whispered in the quietest of whispers.

"Oh, Tamara, I am so sorry you are scared to go to sleep. I will pray for you every night."

"Don't tell me you believed that crock. Hell, my parents didn't even know how to pray," Tamara chuckled.

Sister Ruth appeared at the doorway.

"No talking once lights are out. Those are the rules."

She turned and left, but Tamara could see her shadow outside the door. The nun was listening. It infuriated Tamara.

"I like that Sister Ruth," she announced to her new dorm mates.

"You do? ," they queried.

"Sure I do. She's a straight shooter. Most nuns are sneaky. They prowl around like big old black cats. They listen outside doors. Sister Ruth wouldn't do that."

Tamara knew Sister could hear every word she was saying. She smiled to herself, knowing she had placed the nun in a bind. It might have been okay if Tamara had stopped there, but discretion was never her long suit.

"Hey, have you guys heard the jokes about Johnny, the kid who always got in trouble," asked Tamara.

"No, tell us," whispered the other girls.

And, so, Tamara told every nasty Little Johnny joke she could think of, and then, she shifted gears.

"Here's a great joke. Did you hear about the two nuns who were cleaning the priest's office and found a condom?"

Suddenly, the lights went on, and Sister Ruth stood at the foot of Tamara's bed.

"That's enough, young lady. Get up, and follow me."

The Gym

Sister led Tamara to the gym and told her to sit down in the middle of the large basketball court. She turned off the lights. "You sit here in the dark and pray about your foul mouth and rebellious, sinful attitude. I'll be back later."

Tamara was afraid of the dark, but she wasn't going to let this place get the best of her. She pulled her knees close to her chest, wrapped her arms around them and focused on her anger. She told herself that the rules were silly, that high school girls shouldn't have to go to bed at nine o'clock, and that nuns shouldn't invade people's privacy by listening outside their rooms. But, mostly, she reminded herself how powerless she had felt at FCJ and how she had made a pledge to herself never to feel that powerless again. She told herself that her parents had sent her to this place to break her, and she pledged that no one was going to break her . . . especially Sister Ruth.

The bright lights pulled Tamara out of her angry soliloquy. It was obvious by Sister Ruth's heavy footsteps on the gym floor that her anger had not abated. She glared at Tamara reproachfully.

"Are you ready for an apology?"

"Sister, I've been ready for your apology since you brought me to this gym," Tamara responded sarcastically.

Sister's face became red, she took a deep breath and yelled, "How dare you . . ." Her voice reverberated off the distant walls and startled both of them. Sister stopped in mid-sentence, turned away and held her rosary beads. When she turned around, her anger was under control.

"Do you see that trampoline over there?" Sister pointed to the end of the gym. "That is where you are going to sleep tonight and every night until you apologize to me. I will not have you polluting the minds of the other girls."

Tamara stood up and walked across the floor. She hoped the confidence in her step concealed the alarm in her heart. She climbed onto the trampoline and sat staring at Sister Ruth with eyes of stone. The nun turned off the lights and locked the large doors.

Tamara laid on her side, rolled into the tightest ball possible and began to fight the ghosts that harassed her when she was alone in the dark. She sang songs. She recited poetry. She concocted wild stories of romance and adventure. She cried, and she prayed. She never slept.

By the time Sister returned the next morning, Tamara had decided that apologizing was much easier than spending another night in that terrifying gym. Besides, there would be no witnesses. She could deny having apologized in order to uphold her reputation as the tough, new girl.

No denial was necessary. By the time Tamara joined her classmates at breakfast, everyone had heard some version of the previous night, complete with Tamara's sense of humor and rebellious attitude. Those girls who valued obedience looked at her with disdain. Those girls who valued courage looked at her with admiration. And those girls who valued defiance looked at her with acceptance.

The Misfits

Within days, Tamara connected with a group of misfits who shared two things: an aversion to authority and a desire to not concede their diversity. They shared another strong bond that would slowly surface: they had all experienced adult pain in their young lives. They were assigned to different dorm rooms, but it was impossible to keep them apart.

JILL was an out-spoken atheist. She quit believing in God when her boyfriend of three years was killed by a drunk driver, and her little sister announced, in a confident voice, that he was burning in Hell because he wasn't a Christian.

Jill was not required to attend catechism class at Priory because she wasn't Catholic, but, one day, she agreed to go as Tamara's guest. Tamara promised Jill she would enjoy the class because Father Tom was an enthusiastic teacher who gave interesting lectures and encouraged questions rather than forbade them. Tamara was secretly hoping Jill would challenge Father that day, and she wasn't disappointed.

"Everyone can go to Heaven!" exclaimed Father.

"Not me," contradicted Jill.

"Why not?" asked Father, with a surprised look on his young face.

"Because, I don't believe in Heaven. And, I certainly don't believe in Hell."

"So, what's going to happen to you when you die?" Father asked.

"Guess I'll lie there and rot," Jill shot back.

The girls could not hide their giggles. Father Tom giggled, too.

"Well Jill, I don't want you to lie there and rot, so I am going to pray for you," he said with a smile.

"It won't do any good. I don't believe in prayer either," Jill argued.

"But that's the great thing about prayer," replied Father. "The receiver doesn't have to believe for it to work, just the sender."

It was clear that his response made an impression on Jill. Tamara suspected that Jill was not a true atheist because she was full of anger towards God, and Tamara didn't think you could be that angry at someone you didn't think existed.

PAM'S beauty was evident at an early age. She had flowing blond hair, a peaches and cream complexion and brilliant blue eyes. By sixth grade, she had the shapely figure of a grown woman. Her parents were very religious and determined that Pam would remain virtuous, in spite of her beauty. They were extremely strict and never let her out of the house alone.

But by age fifteen, Pam's sexy appearance and sensual flirting made it clear to everyone, including her parents, that she was experienced with the opposite sex. They demanded an explanation. Her parents were horrified when Pam confessed that her tutors had been friends of her older brother, and the training had taken place in their own home. They sent Pam to Priory with hopes that the chaste atmosphere would restore their daughter's innocence.

Pam arrived at Priory with a box of beauty magazines. She had dreams of being a cosmetologist. Making the misfits beautiful became her mission in life. Tamara was her first assignment.

Tamara had babysat three neighborhood children all summer from noon until five o'clock, Monday through Friday, for seven dollars and fifty cents a week. She had saved every penny and bought contact lenses. She had been fitted with semi-permanent white teeth with gold trim. They were a great improvement over the silver temporaries.

Pam taught Tamara how to wear make-up and how to fix her long, thick hair (which she had refused to cut since her disastrous home perm in seventh grade).

Pam also showed the misfits how to dance, flirt and walk with a teasing confidence that was guaranteed to drive boys crazy. She called it her "Girl Strut."

Tamara was anxious to try out the impact of her new look. She counted the days until she could go home for Thanksgiving vacation and, for once, reality lived up to her expectations. When she strutted into the stadium for the Friday night football game, the girls told her she looked marvelous, and the boys, who had ignored her the previous year, flirted with her all night. The four-day vacation flew by, and she was heartsick when she had to return to Priory.

GUTS (which was short for Guthrie) was tall, thin and agile. She kept everyone in stitches with her physical antics. She was expelled from public school for bad grades. Ironically, Guts studied harder than any of the misfits, but every class was a struggle for her. Years later, it would, undoubtedly, become obvious that Guts suffered from a learning disability, but in the 1960's such kids were labeled lazy and stupid and were encouraged to quit school.

Tamara discovered that Guts did better if she studied out loud, so they snuck into the bathroom late at night and prepared for tests together. Everyone celebrated when Guts achieved a "C" average because that meant she could join them for their monthly trip to town on Saturday afternoon.

Passing grades and an approved excuse were required before the girls were permitted to ride the Priory school bus into town.

Acceptable excuses were doctor appointments and necessary shopping. There was a small store at Priory which sold snacks, school supplies, and toiletries, but it didn't carry sanitary napkins or tampons. Tamara thought it was silly for a girl's school to not have sanitary supplies, but no one complained because that meant at least once a month the girls had an acceptable excuse to go shopping in town.

Priory girls were required to wear dresses. It was a requirement the misfits hated because it immediately identified them to the town kids. It was Guts who solved the problem. They rolled up slacks under their skirts. As soon as the bus departed, they went to the drug store bathroom, removed their skirts and hid them in a paper bag behind the trash can. They changed back into their skirts just in time to catch the return bus to school three hours later.

PAULINE was sick a lot. She had had an ulcer since grade school. She was quiet and solemn. A week before Christmas break, she trusted the misfits enough to tell her story. She spoke in a soft voice, void of emotion.

Her father was a mean, violent alcoholic. Her mother suffered shattered bones and broken teeth at his hands but refused to leave him because she had no way to support her daughters. One night he came into Pauline's bedroom. He was drunk. He fell down on top of her. She screamed and slapped his face. Her mother rushed into the room and pounded him on the back. He stood, turned and unleashed his rage on his wife. When Pauline tried to protect her mother, he punched his daughter in the face.

She fell, hitting her head on the corner of the dresser. An ambulance took her to the hospital. She was unconscious for days. The incident left her with seizures, excruciating headaches and an embarrassing stutter.

"The s-s-social worker threatened to p-p-put me in a foster home so they s-s-sent me to P-p-priory," finished Pauline.

The misfits were overwhelmed with sadness for their friend. It seemed an eternity before anyone spoke. Tamara broke the awkward silence.

"Well, I for one am glad you are here and not around that sick son-of-a . . .."

"N-N-No," interrupted Pauline, shaking her head, "I should be home to protect my m-m-mother and s-s-sister."

"But, that isn't your job," protested Guts.

"Yes, it is," insisted Pauline. She continued in a halting voice. "It was my f-f-fault. It's all my f-f-fault."

"How could it be your fault? You didn't do anything wrong. What sense does that make?" asked Pam.

Tamara saw the futile look in Pauline's eyes and decided it was time to rescue her friend.

"It makes perfect sense to me," she said loudly.

"Why?" Guts inquired.

"Because, we are Catholic, and Catholics feel guilty about everything."

"Atheists don't feel guilty," bragged Jill.

"I'm Catholic, and I've never felt guilty about anything," asserted Pam.

"Oh, come on, Pam," challenged Tamara. "You can't expect us to believe you don't feel guilty about all the fun you've had with boys."

"Nope, I just go to confession. That's the best thing about being Catholic," chuckled Pam. "I just seek forgiveness, instead of asking permission."

Laughter lifted the heavy mood of sadness from the room.
Later that night when the girls were laying alone in their beds,
they recalled Pauline's story and their own burdens seemed
suddenly lighter.

The Chapel

That was one of the many nights when Tamara left her bed
and crept down the long, dark hallways to the immense
chapel. She sat in the back corner with her shoulders pressed
against the wall. She stared at the small candle flickering on
the altar. The nuns said the candle was a sign of God's presence, but she didn't need a candle to feel God in this majestic,
holy place.

Tamara was afraid of God. She believed Him to be powerful,
demanding and quick to punish. She never prayed directly to
God. She had been taught that Mary, the Mother of Jesus,
had special standing in the eyes of God and could intercede
for children. Tamara took her prayers directly to Mary.

That night Tamara began her prayers as she always did, by
confessing her rebellious nature. She asked Mary to tell God
that she was truly sorry for all the things she did wrong and
would try hard to be a better person. That night she also
asked Mary to protect Pauline, and, as she did so, her eyes
filled with tears.

While the other girls had felt sympathy for Pauline, Tamara
had felt empathy. Like Pauline, Tamara believed she was
somehow responsible for everything bad that happened to
herself and to those she loved. During the day, the burden of
carrying all the blame for the world's problems made her
angry. But at night, alone in the dark, she felt only helplessness and fear. That is why she came to the chapel seeking
comfort and forgiveness.

The Last of the Misfits

SUSAN had been overweight since grade school. Fat kids are
the universal targets of cruelty on school playgrounds. Susan

had gotten pretty good at pretending the attacks didn't bother her, but the misfits knew better. They realized every jeer and joke chipped away at Susan's fragile self-esteem, so they made it clear that teasing Susan at Priory was off-limits.

Susan had one amazing talent. She could fart on demand. Adults couldn't appreciate that talent, but to teenagers, it was an amazing gift, indeed. Susan had great comedic timing and knew just the moment to utilize her talent in order to create waves of laughter among the girls. The nuns suspected that Susan did it on purpose, but the embarrassment that immediately crossed her face was very convincing. They could hardly punish her for a simple (albeit gross) breach of etiquette.

Susan was mischievous and creative. She was forever inventing ways to break the boredom and rules at Priory. It was her idea to explore the laundry. Goal–to discover if nuns really used rags instead of Kotex. (They didn't.) It was her idea to"accidentally" pull Sister Ruth's head piece off while sledding. Goal– to see if nuns really shaved their heads. (They didn't.) And, it was her idea to invade the kitchen one Saturday night.

Guts had no problem picking the refrigerator lock with a hairpin, and to everyone's delight, they discovered a large bucket of chocolate ice cream. They devoured the treat and buried the bucket outside. They would have gotten away with their theft if Linda, the ultimate tattle-tale, hadn't overhead them talking about it and reported them to Sister Ruth. As a punishment, they were not allowed to go to town that month. They were furious. Linda was a snitch and retaliation was clearly called for.

Mischief

The nuns congregated in the chapel for prayers every evening, and for one hour, the girls were left unsupervised. Most of the girls studied in their rooms. The misfits always met in the break room.

The night for retribution against Linda arrived. As soon as she went into the shower, the misfits went into action. They carried their mattresses outside and piled them in the snow. Then, they carried Linda's mattress into the bathroom and threw it over the shower stall onto her head. The misfits dashed back to their chairs in the break room. Linda's screams brought the nuns running. Minutes later, Sister Ruth stormed into the break room.

"How could you do such a mean thing? she shouted at the misfits. "You scared Linda to death."

They looked at Sister innocently.

"We don't know what you are talking about. We heard screams, but we didn't do anything."

"Don't give me that," disputed Sister Ruth. "This group is behind every bit of trouble that goes on here. Now get to your rooms."

The girls walked to their separate dorm rooms with the sad faces of those who were unable to prove their innocence. Moments later, each girl rushed back into the hall yelling, "Sister Ruth, my mattress is gone!!"

The long search for the missing mattresses ended when someone spotted them outside. Sister Ruth apologized profusely for accusing the misfits earlier. It was clear that whoever threw Linda's mattress into the shower, also put the mattresses out in the snow. It never occurred to Sister that the misfits had done both, in order to cast blame elsewhere.

The mattresses were too wet to sleep on, so, the girls spent the night together in sleeping bags on the gym floor. They congratulated themselves on a successful strategy. Pam told them how to kiss boys, and they practiced on the back of their hands. They giggled all night.

Their next escapade was not so successful.

They snuck into the break room late one Saturday night with the intention of raiding the pop machine. Susan had a plan. She was convinced they could use a can opener to pop the tops off the bottles while they were in the machine, tip them forward and empty the contents into a glass. It worked like a charm. They were so inspired by this discovery, that they worked on the candy machine until they found a way to reach up inside and release candy bars without paying.

When the half empty bottles were detected, Sister Ruth complained to the vendor that the bottles had leaked. However, closer inspection revealed an empty candy machine and a noticeable absence of coins. It was clear there had been a theft.

A search of the dorm floor uncovered candy wrappings in Susan's trash and uneaten candy bars in Guts' closet. The misfits had a code of loyalty, so once the two girls were caught, the rest quickly confessed. Sister Ruth assembled them in her office and gave them a lecture about the evils of stealing. Then, she spelled out their punishment. "You will not be allowed to go to town for the Symphony Christmas concert Saturday night. When the other girls board the buses for town, you will be confined to your rooms."

Disappointment was evident on their faces. The Christmas concert was the only night-time outing planned for the year. The girls had discussed nothing else for weeks. Pam had purchased a new dress. Guts had agreed to wear make-up. Even Pauline had expressed excitement about the trip. Sister's announcement had the desired impact on the girls. They hung their heads and, for once, showed no defiance.

"However," Sister Ruth announced, "I could be persuaded to change my mind and let you go."

Each girl looked at Sister. She could see the hope in their stares. Sister thought to herself, *Now I have your undivided attention.*

"Many of the other nuns think you are bad girls," she continued in a solemn voice. "Some even think you are beyond saving. I don't agree." She paused dramatically, and then continued,"But it is clear that you bring out the worst in each other. You may go to the concert Saturday night if you agree to break up this little group of yours."

The girls were stunned. They expected to be punished, but this proposition caught them totally off guard. Each girl thought the proposal was absurd, but no one wanted to be presumptuous and speak for the others. Each girl began to wonder if the others would think the trade-off a fair one. Sister Ruth scanned them with satisfaction. It was clear their loyalty and confidence was faltering.

"Well," Sister asked, "what will it be? This clique or the concert?"

No one said a word. Sister Ruth was becoming impatient.

"I am only going to ask you one more time. Will you agree not to talk to each other the rest of the year? Someone say something, now."

And then it happened. Susan farted. Not just a small, quiet fart. Oh, no! This was a whopper. Record volume. Record endurance. The misfits lost it. First they smiled. Then they giggled. Finally, they let loose with all-out guffaws until their eyes overflowed with tears. Sister kept yelling for them to stop, but it was no use. The hysterics were beyond their control.

Needless to say, they didn't get to go to town for the performance of the symphony. When they stood at their respective dorm windows watching the other students excitedly board the buses, they did feel some regret. But, no one mentioned it at the time. Instead, they assembled in the infirmary, their favorite hiding place, and Susan taught them all how to fart on demand.

Lent

Christmas break came and went with astounding speed, and the girls returned to school for second semester. The post-holiday mood at Priory was heavy. Even the most conscientious students found it difficult to study. The gloom was especially noticeable amongst the misfits. They seldom talked and almost never laughed. Tamara spent many nights in the chapel.

The beginning of Lent lifted everyone's spirits because it marked the nearing of Easter break. The girls were required to give up dessert for Lent. Tamara complained loudly at every meal, but it wasn't the ban on sweets that made her angry. It was the Lenten season. Purple cloths were draped over all the statues and crucifixes in the building. The nuns talked incessantly about the torture Jesus endured and how sinful men had killed Him. Tamara wanted to stand up and shout, "Stop blaming me. I didn't crucify Jesus. I wasn't even there." But she never protested because she knew in her heart that she was a bad kid, and if she had been born in the time of Jesus, she would have been guilty of something.

One week before Easter break, Pauline was called home. Her mother was in the hospital. Two days later, Sister Ruth announced at mass that Pauline wasn't returning to Priory because she was sick. She asked the students to pray for Pauline. Everyone bowed their heads.

"She isn't sick," Tamara overheard Linda say. "When I called my mother last night, she said Pauline tried to kill herself. A lady at her church said that she slit her wrists. Isn't that gross?"

"Yeah, but I'm not s-s-surprised," whispered Linda's friend, with a mocking stutter. "S-s-she was s-s-so weird."

They covered their mouths to muffle their giggles. For a moment, Tamara was overcome with shock. Then her rage emerged. She stood up and snapped at the surprised girls behind her.

"You bitches wouldn't know weird if you tripped over it."

Tamara exited the pew. Noticing her departure, Sister Ruth rushed up.

"Are you sick Tamara?"

"Yes," she shouted, "sick of this place. Sick of the prayers. And, sick of those ugly purple drapes covering everything."

"Those drapes are to remind us of the suffering of Our Lord."

"How about the suffering of people," interrupted Tamara. "Doesn't that count? You don't even care about the suffering that goes on around here. You just hide behind those purple drapes and pretend everything is fine. Well, it isn't fine."

"Sit down, right now," demanded Sister.

Tamara ignored her and ran down the aisle.

"If you don't come back, you will be sorry," Sister Ruth shouted as Tamara exited the chapel.

Tamara raced out of the building and cut across the open fields. She ran until her lungs felt as though they would explode through her chest. She ran until her legs ached and head throbbed. She was grateful for the pain in her body. It took the focus off her breaking heart. When she could run no more, she walked in a daze. The sun was setting when she reached the edge of town. She saw a police car approaching and realized she was wearing her uniform. She ducked behind a tree, and then dodged down side streets and alleys until she found herself in the heart of downtown.

Finding the Answer

It was dark. She was frightened and alone. Then, she saw the cathedral. It was an imposing building but the bright lights shining through the stained glass windows seemed warm and inviting. She entered quietly and knelt down. A middle-aged couple stared. It made her nervous. She decided she would be less conspicuous if she had a reason for being in church. She approached the confessionals but they were empty. Then she saw an elderly woman doing the stations of the cross.

The stations were pictures depicting the major events of the crucifixion. Tamara had always refused to do the stations because they seemed morbid to her. At this moment, they seemed like the perfect decoy.

She walked to the first picture, genuflected and made the sign of the cross. She studied the etching. It was beautifully done. It was so large that she could see the face of Jesus. He had kind eyes. She went to the next picture. Once again, she was drawn to the eyes which reflected warmth and acceptance. She was mesmerized. She saw something in these pictures she had never seen before. She saw a loving God.

When she studied the depiction of Jesus abandoned by his sleeping friends the night before his painful death, she felt His loneliness. When she approached the vivid depiction of the crown of thorns being forced onto His head, she felt His humiliation. When she forced herself to look into the eyes of the soldiers whipping His bare back, she felt His pain. Tears were stinging her eyes.

By the time she reached the crucifixion, she was sobbing into her folded hands, for she knew that God understood the rejection and pain that she and Pauline and the misfits had felt, for He had once felt it too. And, when she stood at the last station and saw the open arms and sparkling eyes of Jesus as he ascended into heaven, she knew with certainty that God loved her.

Tamara felt a tap on her shoulder. She spun around and found herself gazing into the soft eyes of the elderly woman who had been finishing the stations when Tamara started.

"I want to thank you for the Easter gift you have given me," she whispered to Tamara in the sweetest of voices. "I have spent the last hour watching you. I have never seen anyone do the stations with such intensity. You see dear, when you have been praying as long as I have, devotionals have a tendency to get routine, even bland. But, tonight, your tears reminded me of the magnitude of God's sacrifice. Thank you for allowing me to share your gift of passion."

Tamara felt like a hypocrite. She didn't deserve the praise of this kind woman. For it was her own pain, not God's, that had brought tears to her eyes. Tamara could not let the deception continue.

"But, you don't understand," Tamara protested. "When I did it, I was only thinking of me."

"I do understand," the lady said with a twinkling in her eye, "and when God did it, He was only thinking of you." The lady left the cathedral with a smile on her face.

Tamara scanned the building and was relieved to discover that she was alone. Suddenly she felt exhausted. She laid down on the back pew and fell asleep thinking of the old lady's kind words.

Father Tom

She sat up with a start. Someone was shaking her. Sunlight was pouring in the windows. When her eyes cleared, she saw the warm face of Father Tom.

"The janitor told me he spotted someone sleeping here. When he described the clothes, I knew it was a Priory uniform. No one would wear those colors by choice." Tamara couldn't help but laugh.

"I had a call from Sister Ruth last evening reporting you had run away. She is pretty worried about you."

"Oh, yeah, and I bet she didn't sleep a wink," Tamara murmured.

"And, your friends are so worried that they spent the night in the chapel. They have refused to leave."

"The misfits – in church – by choice . . . ." Tamara responded with a look of amazement. "Well, I'll be damned."

"Let's hope not," said Father. "So, why don't you tell me what happened to make you take such desperate action."

Tamara started to respond, "Nothing," but the sincerity in Father's eyes dissolved her tough facade. She felt her eyes fill with tears as she told him about Pauline and the girls who had mocked her stutter. Then, she found herself sharing her own loneliness and fears. He listened intently, and they talked for a long time.

"Are you hungry?" Father Tom asked.

"I'm starving."

"Let's go to the rectory, and I'll make you some toast while I call the hospital and see if Pauline is okay. I'll call Mother Superior and tell her I found you."

"Don't call her," pleaded Tamara. "I will get into so much trouble."

"No, you won't. I'll tell her that they mustn't punish you because you had a very good reason for your behavior."

"Mother Superior won't listen to you."

"Sure she will," he winked. "I may be half her age, but I say the mass at Priory twice a week, and I'll threaten to cut them off if she doesn't do what I say."

His easy laugh gave Tamara confidence. Father Tom was true to his word. He drove Tamara back to Priory and while she waited in the car, he had a long discussion with Sister Ruth. When he finally signaled for her to get out of the car, Sister Ruth merely smiled and said, "Welcome back Tamara. We praise God you are not hurt."

Father Tom put his hand on Tamara's shoulder and said softly, "From now on I want you to remember, you aren't alone. There will always be people you can talk to. Just give them a chance. Now, why don't you go to the chapel and show that gang of yours that you are okay. My guess is they are getting claustrophobic in there."

"Especially Jill," smiled Tamara.

"Oh, yes, your friend the atheist. She has been stuck in church for twelve hours with nothing to do but pray," Father chuckled. "See Tamara, something good comes out of everything."

Tamara couldn't help but laugh when she walked into the chapel and saw the misfits sitting in silent prayer.

"So," Tamara called out, "Have you guys gone soft on me. Are you going to become nuns?"

"Sounds good," said Susan, "I hear those habits are 'one-size-fits-all.'"

"Yes," protested Pam, "but they'll have to let me wear blue instead of black to show off my eyes."

"And, they'll have to call me Sister Guts."

Tamara turned to Jill, "What about you?"

Jill grinned, "Not me, I was just in here 'cuz it got me out of geometry class."

The girls gathered around, and Tamara shared her adventure of the previous night. They were visibly relieved when she told them Pauline was going to be all right. They walked out of the chapel with their arms around each other and their heads held high.

The weeks after Easter break flew by and soon it was time to leave. Sister Ruth informed the misfits that they would not be welcome back at Priory the next year because they were not compatible with the program. The parents were disappointed. The girls were thrilled.

Back Home

When Tamara returned home everything was pretty much the same. Her parents were seriously threatening divorce and Tamara suspected a separation would be laden with the same malice that marred their marriage. Tamara immediately resurrected her protective wall of anger and defiance.

Tamara also found a new way to escape the stress at home: she buried herself in activities. She also discovered that performing was the perfect outlet for her intensity and energy. She joined the high school speech team, took voice lessons, sang in three choirs, earned the lead in the school musical, organized a folk singing group and competed in the local Miss America Pageant. She also kept her grades high and qualified for the National Honor Society. In order to alleviate the financial pressures of her parent's impending divorce, she got a job at a clothing store evenings and weekends. Unfortunately, the pattern of avoiding problems by staying busy would haunt her for life.

She never heard from her friends at Priory again but she often recalled their laughing faces and the wild adventures they had shared. The memories made her smile.

"My parents sent me to finishing school in North Dakota," she would joke to her friends. "I finished off two nuns and a priest." Priory had been a positive experience. She had learned to study, dance, use make-up, pray and, of course, fart on demand. The misfits had given her a gift. They had shown her that there were other teenagers who had been hurt by life and were choosing to fight back. They had helped her realize–she was a survivor.

And a strong piece of glass was put into place

The Lesson

God Cares

The most important lesson I learned from my experience at Priory is that God cares. It is truly ironic that I discovered how much I needed God in the year of my greatest rebellion. I guess I shouldn't have been surprised. After all, Jesus was a rebel, as was Peter, as was Paul.

There is a longing in our hearts to know God and to grow spiritually. There are times in our lives when that need is over-shadowed by busy schedules, financial pursuits, and relationship demands. There are times when that need is muffled by egotism and intellectual arrogance. But, eventually, we all discover that physical rewards are shallow and fleeting. Eventually, all of us ask the same questions: "What do I believe?" and "What values provide stability in my life?"

My Catholic upbringing was an asset in my spiritual journey because it gave me a certainty of God at an early age. The teachings of the Catholic church in the fifties and sixties were also a liability because they focused on a God of vengeance, rather than a God of love. As a child, I had a clear image of God as an angry, disappointed deity who tracked the transgressions of people, carefully calculating the perfect punishment for each sin. Even the crucifixion represented failure and death.

It was at Priory that I made the powerful discovery that God is a loving God. The closer I got to His love, the more I realized the crucifixion represented life, not death. It represented freedom, not slavery. It represented peace, not guilt.

My walk with God has not been an easy walk. I am, after all, a rebel at heart. There have been times when I rejected God because I saw Him as a crutch for those who didn't have the courage to walk through life without a safety net.

There have been times when I denied God because, as an intellectual, I decided a belief in God was for inferior thinkers. I discovered at FCJ and Priory that when I was forced to focus, I have a sharp mind. But, viewing oneself as an intellectual can be a trap of pride and deception. It gives a false sense of control and superiority. That is not to say that spiritual pursuits are void of contemplation and inquiry. A review of history confirms that most scholars and leaders professed a strong belief in God, and, also, candidly confessed to an ongoing struggle between balancing self-reliance and faith.

Those times when I thought I was too strong or too smart for God were the loneliest, most difficult times in my life. Yet I continue to make those mistakes. I have a strong personality. I fight the tendency daily to rely totally on myself. I begin each day by sincerely asking God for guidance. By mid-morning, I suggest to God that I am doing fine on my own, and I'll give Him a call if I need anything. At bedtime, I angrily demand, "Where were You today when I needed You?"

My walk with God has also been hampered by the pursuit of religion rather than the pursuit of God. There were times when I validated my choice of religion by declaring myself right and others wrong. Each time, God convicted me that such thinking was not only arrogant but hazardous to my own spiritual growth. I am a fighter by nature, so it will always be a struggle for me to reconcile my need to speak out against injustice with the commandment not to judge.

God is a big God. He values diversity and enables people to find Him in a myriad of ways. God is a fair God and He will reveal His path to anyone who seeks directions. After all, finding God is not like playing a game of "Let's Make A Deal." We are not nervous contestants, trying to pick the right door.

"I choose door number one."

"Sorry, wrong choice," snickers an all-knowing emcee. "God was hiding behind door number two. Your booby prize is eternal damnation."

God values freedom of choice and will not force Himself on anyone. God's voice is a voice of love and hope. It is a soft voice, not a forceful one. It is always there, but it does not push itself into our lives. There is an unlocked door between us and God. The handle is on our side. God waits patiently to be invited in.

Angels

God also places angels in our paths to provide encourage-ment, enlightenment and guidance. At Priory, Father Tom and the elderly lady in the cathedral were God's angels. At FCJ, the doctor was an angel, as was the skater, and, of course, Elizabeth, my hospital roommate. Even when I was assaulted in the alley as a child, God was there. He helped me bury the pain. And, when the time was right for me to recall and process the painful memories, He put angels in my path who wrapped me in love.

If you recall the difficult challenges you have faced in your life, you too will discover angels. They were there sharing words of wisdom, offering hugs, and preventing you from making bad decisions. They wrapped you in the warmth of kindness when you felt the chill of rejection.

There have been times when God has called you to be an angel for someone else. You felt a strong urging to call, write, or stop by and see someone. Each time you followed that urging you were received with the confirming words, "How did you know I needed you today?"

Sometimes we do not appreciate God's angels because we are blinded by pain and cynicism, but they are there. They have always been there, and they always will be. As will God because He loves us. We are not alone.

People often approach me after my speeches and ask, "How did you endure all your struggles?"

The answer is simple. It is the lesson from this chapter:

- ⊛ God has guided me.
- ⊛ God has strengthened me.
- ⊛ God has carried me.
- ⊛ God has never abandoned me, even when I abandoned Him.

When Life Kicks—Kick Back

Chapter Six
Bad Choices

By the time Tamara was seventeen, she had perfected the ability to be tough and independent. That's why it is surprising that she entered an abusive relationship.

Tamara knew that she was attracted to the wrong men. She liked those who had a reputation for being unattainable and egotistical. She was amazed at how easy it was to manipulate men. All it required was carefully rationed passion and promises of more to come. It was a game to her, like fishing. She would cast the bait, hook the fish and reel it in. She didn't keep the fish. It was definitely a game of "catch and release." She always cut the line before they could hurt her. The danger was obvious. Eventually, she was bound to hook a shark.

Dale—The Beginning

Dale was a college student. He was tall and good-looking. He owned a house, drove an expensive car, and threw the best parties in town. He dated beautiful girls, but rumor had it, he didn't commit. Tamara planned to change that. She went to a party at his house and flirted with him all evening, ignoring the embarrassment of her date and the hostility of his. It worked. He asked her out.

When Dale arrived for their first date, he spent twenty minutes fawning over her mother. Kay was delighted. Tamara was disgusted.

"Would it be okay with you if I took Tamara shopping before dinner? I want to buy her a new dress that will always remind her of our first date," asked Dale, as he smiled at Kay.

"What a lovely thought," responded Kay.

"Mother," interrupted Tamara, "don't answer for me. I think it's a dumb idea."

"Would you excuse us, Dale? Tamara and I need to talk in the kitchen," replied a smiling Kay.

Tamara stomped out of the room. Before Kay followed, she whispered to Dale, "Tamara is very stubborn. She can be quite a handful you know." Dale shook his head in sympathy. "I understand, but I promise you, I can handle her."

"What do you think you are doing? Dale is the nicest young man you have ever dated," snapped Kay once they were in the kitchen.

"Why, Mother," queried Tamara, her voice laden with sarcasm, "because he drives an expensive car, wears expensive clothes? It couldn't be the fact that he has money that makes him so 'nice,' could it, Mother?"

"Don't use that tone with me, Tamara, and don't act so self-righteous. There is nothing wrong with having money. Let him buy you a dress. After all," Kay snickered, "it's never too early to get a man in the habit of spending money on you. Trust me, it makes life and love more tolerable."

Tamara was tempted to break her date with Dale just to spite her mother, but he was good-looking and popular. Tamara couldn't wait to be seen with him. She walked back into the living room and smiled at Dale, "Let's get going. I'm starved." Dale stood up. He was a full ten inches taller than Tamara. "The restaurant is right by the mall, so I can buy you a new dress and show you off." Tamara started to protest, but decided against arguing with Dale on their first date. "That sounds good," she surrendered. Had Tamara realized the dangerous path she had just stepped onto, she would not have given in so easily.

Dale—The Manipulator

Tamara loved to watch Dale manipulate people. He charmed everyone, especially her mother. Kay allowed them to date on school nights because in her own words, "Dale was the man every mother wanted for her daughter."

Tamara took perverse pleasure in Kay's gullibility. In reality, Dale was the most reckless guy she had ever dated. He bought her a fake I.D., so they could go to bars. There was a party at his house every weekend with kegs of beer and bags of junk food. Party crashers were welcome. Tamara thought it peculiar that Dale didn't have any real friends—just an endless string of strangers who ate his food and drank his booze.

Dale—The Controller

At first, Dale was the perfect boyfriend. Then his jealousy and need to control began to surface. It happened slowly. He insisted she wear a certain perfume. He told her which clothes looked best on her. He wanted her to listen to his favorite music because hers was juvenile. He demanded Tamara stop hanging around with her friends.

"They're just dumb high school girls."

"They aren't dumb," she protested.

"Sure, Baby, they aren't dumb, just young. You act so much older than they do."

He told her not to talk to other guys.

"They need to know you belong to me."

"I don't belong to anyone," snapped Tamara.

"Of course not, Baby," cooed Dale, "but they flirt with you just to hurt me. You don't want to embarrass me, do you?"

She understood hurt and embarrassment, so she nodded in agreement. He wrapped his huge arms around her, "Just remember, Baby, we don't need anyone. We've got each other."

A little voice in the back of her head warned that he was too possessive, but she rationalized that his jealousy proved his love. *I'm learning a lot,* she told herself. *I'm learning what makes women beautiful—what men like.*

Sometimes, she missed her friends and the activities at high school. But, she had always been good at rationalizing, and this situation was no different. And, besides, deep in her heart she believed she could control him. It was just a matter of carefully allocating affection.

Tamara misjudged Dale. He didn't like her games. He wasn't patient. He demanded more. Tamara decided it was time to prove that she couldn't be bullied. She stood him up on their next date. She left to go to a movie and pizza with her friends, Marsha, Shirley and Sharon an hour before Dale arrived.

Tamara had forgotten how much she laughed with her friends. They found humor in silly things. They ate pizza and talked about their plans after graduation. It was a relaxing evening. When they dropped her off at her house, Marsha rolled down the car window and yelled, "See you tomorrow–noon–The Frost Top. Be there, or be square." Tamara shouted back. "I'll be there."

As she turned and walked up the sidewalk, she was smiling. Tamara was happier than she had been in months. She thought about Dale for the first time all evening, and her smile disappeared. Suddenly she felt cold. She wrapped her arms around herself and looked at the bright stars that dotted the midnight sky. "It is time to cut him loose," she whispered to herself. An angry voice came from the front porch, "Where have you been?" Tamara spun around, startled to see Dale standing in the shadows.

"Dale . . . I didn't know you were here . . . I didn't see your car."

"I parked it around the corner."

"Why?"

He ignored her question. His voice was cold and controlled, "Where have you been?"

Tamara's words displayed more courage than her voice. "That's really none of your business."

"Everything you do is my business—where you go—who you are with. It's all my business."

Anger gave Tamara confidence. Her voice was stronger, "In your dreams. You don't own me."

"I own you," he snarled. "I have the bills to prove it. I've spent plenty on you."

"You can have it all back. I don't want your junk."

Suddenly he was holding her shoulders and glaring into her face.

"Stop acting like a spoiled child. Sit down. I want to talk to you."

"I don't want to talk."

"Don't talk . . . just listen."

Dale pushed her forward onto the porch steps. He didn't speak for several minutes. He paced. Tamara wanted to leave, but something warned her not to upset him further. When he finally spoke, his voice was menacing.

"I did a lot of thinking tonight. I've been pushing you too hard. I can see that now. You're still just a kid . . ."

"I'm not a kid . . .," she began to protest, but his sharp glare silenced her.

"Fine, you're not a kid. Anyway, I'll slow down. We'll take this at your pace. I decided that tonight. I was thinking about you with some other guy, and it made me crazy."

"I wasn't with some other guy. I went to a movie and pizza with my friends."

"I hope it was worth skipping our date for." challenged Dale sarcastically.

"I had a very nice time," she began, all the while ignoring his sarcasm. " We laughed and talked. It was good seeing them again. Sharon got the scholarship she wanted, and Marsha broke up with Darrel, and . . ."

"Yeah, whatever" he interrupted. "The point is, I've been pushing you . . ."

"You've been smothering me," she broke in.

"Yeah, whatever. Anyway, I'll lighten up."

He turned and walked down the sidewalk.

"I'll pick you up tomorrow. Wear that red top, the cropped one . . ."

"I can't go," she asserted.

He whipped around and glared at her.

"I . . . I told the girls I'd meet them for lunch," she said hesitantly, "and tomorrow night we're going to the Beacon for a Senior dance. It might be our last chance to be together."

He took a slow, deliberate step towards her. The porch light caught the rage in his eyes. His voice seethed with anger.

"You didn't ask me what I did tonight while you were out with your little high school buddies. I spent the evening with Ralph and Sam. You remember Ralph and Sam, don't you?"

"How could I forget them. They're weird," she mumbled. His scowl stopped her from saying more.

"Yeah, but they know how to get your mind off a stupid girl. They picked up some cats from the dog pound, so we could play games."

"What kind of games?" Tamara asked hesitantly.

"We put them in bottles, threw them in the lake and bet which one would sink first. We tied bricks to their necks and raced them. We even tied firecrackers to a couple of them."

"That's sick," she responded in shock.

"Whatever. I wouldn't have gone if you'd been here for our date. It was your fault I hooked up with those guys. When your mother said you weren't here, I got mad, real mad. I had to do something with the anger. That sorta makes it your fault, doesn't it? When I'm mad, I gotta take it out on someone." He paused and let the words sink in before finishing, "I'll be here at seven. Wear that short black skirt I bought you, the tight one."

Tamara was going to protest, but his sinister smile stopped her cold. She turned and went into the house.

The next day she met her friends at the Frost Top and told them what Dale had done the night before.

"The poor cats," sighed Sharon.

"That's so evil," counseled Marsha.

"Dale's dangerous," warned Shirley. "You've got to break up with him."

"How?" asked Tamara. "He scares me. I don't want to talk to him."

"You don't have to talk to him," responded Shirley. "When I drove by he was mowing his lawn. We'll drive over there right now, and you throw his ring out the car window. Even someone as dense as Dale will get the meaning of that."

Marsha and Sharon laughed. Tamara joined in.

Twenty minutes later, Shirley drove into his driveway and honked the horn. When Dale turned, Tamara hurled his ring as hard as she could. Her aim was good. She hit him in the forehead. Shirley left black tire tracks as they sped away. The girls' laughter could be heard for a block. Tamara would not have been laughing if she had seen the rage in Dale's eyes.

Dale—The Terrorizer

That night she went to the Beacon with her friends. The Beacon was an old nightclub that had a live band on weekends. They did not serve alcohol. It was always packed with young kids. Neighbors were often threatening to close it down because of the noise and the drinking in the parking lot, but for now, it was open, and Tamara was happy to be there. She felt free. She closed her eyes and danced to the loud music.

Suddenly, Marsha was shaking her, "You gotta get out of here. Dale is looking for you, and he's drunk." Before she took two steps, Dale's strong arms grabbed her from behind. In one effortless motion he threw her over his shoulder and began to spin her around the dance floor. "Let me go. Help me," she screamed.

No one could hear her over the pounding drums and loud guitars. She pummeled his back with her fists, but he didn't flinch. The rowdy crowd began to cheer. The harder she fought, the more they cheered. Dale waved his free hand and took a bow. Someone yelled, "Go, Dale!", and soon everyone picked up the chant. The crowd thought it was a game, but

Tamara knew better. She knew she was in serious trouble. He carried her out of the old building with the chant echoing in her ears. "Go, Dale! Go, Dale!"

He opened the driver's side of a dilapidated old car and threw her across the seat. Before she could sit up, he was beside her. She tried to open the passenger door. He grabbed her hair and pulled her to him.

"You're hurting me," she cried.

"Not as much as you hurt me."

"Please, let go of my hair. I won't try to open the door again."

He released her hair and grabbed her neck. With his free hand he started the car and sped out of the parking lot. Gravel spit out behind them.

"Slow down," she yelled. "You're going to kill us."

"Shut up!" he snapped.

Tamara knew she was in a position of weakness. She sat quietly and tried to think what to do next.

"You can't break up with me. You can never leave me. Do you hear me?" he threatened.

"You don't even like me," she mumbled.

"How can you say something so stupid?" Dale asked as he squeezed her neck.

"It's not stupid. You try to change everything about me. My clothes, my hair, my friends . . ."

"I just want you to be the best. With my help you could be anything, but you're such an ingrate."

He pushed his foot down hard on the gas pedal He was taking the curves much too fast.

"You're going to wreck this car."

"I don't care. It isn't mine."

"Where did you get it?"

"From a couple of drunks outside the Crystal Bar. I waved a one hundred dollar bill in front of them and said I'd have it back in a few hours." He laughed.

He drove to the top of the Rimrocks, a butte that bordered the city. It was a popular place for passionate teenagers. The lights of the entire valley could be seen sparkling below. Dale drove dangerously close to the edge. He pulled her to his chest and whispered in her ear.

"I'm going to drive off the cliff. We're going to die together."

"Don't, please, don't," she pleaded in a voice made small and breathless by her fear, "I promise I won't break up with you."

"It's too late for that," he asserted as he revved the engine.

"Dale, I'm not good enough for you," Tamara stated in an attempt to divert his attention. "You were right when you said I'm just a kid. You deserve someone more mature, someone with more class."

"I don't want anyone else. We belong together. If I can't have you, no one can," his voice crackling with anger.

"I'm not worth dying for," she asserted, hoping against hope that her strategy wouldn't backfire.

"You're right about that," he snarled.

He took his foot off the gas pedal. Minutes passed. He seemed to be weighing her comments. Suddenly, he backed up the car and sped down the highway towards town. He drove over a sidewalk and into a city park.

"Remember this park," he quizzed.

"Of course, it's where you kissed me for the first time. On the swing set. It was sweet."

"It's the first place I bring every date," Dale snickered. "You women are so gullible."

His new tone was cold and unemotional. It scared her worse than his outrage.

"Please, Dale, let me go."

"Fine, if you want out of my life, get out of my life."

Dale reached over, opened the passenger door and began pushing her from the speeding car.

"Get out," he yelled.

"I can't get out if the car is moving."

"Sure you can."

He laughed and shoved his foot harder against the gas pedal. He drove through bushes. He used one hand to steer the car towards a clump of full grown trees and the other to push her towards the door. Tamara was terrified. She was grasping for something to hold onto–anything. She was hanging out of the car from the waist down, and she felt bushes scrapping her legs. She knew the trees were close. She knew the open door would hit one of those trees, slam shut, and sever her legs. The gruesome thought gave her extra strength.

She grabbed onto his arm and pulled herself up. She reached the steering wheel. It took all her strength to swing her body into the moving car. Seconds later, the open door crashed into a large oak tree. The explosion of crushing metal was deafening. The door slammed shut with such force, it shook the car.

"You almost killed me!" Tamara screamed. "You're crazy! You're so crazy!"

"Shut up," Dale yelled and punched her head.   Tamara was so numb with fear that she couldn't feel his blows. As he turned a sharp corner, the smashed car door swung open. It hit a parked car and slammed shut. Once again, she thought of how close she had come to losing her legs. She shuddered. He stopped hitting her as he approached downtown because he needed two hands to maneuver through the busy Saturday night traffic. He slowed as he approached a stoplight.

Tamara realized this was her last chance. She kicked open the door and pushed against his legs. Before he could stop her, she was out of the car. She ran behind the car and down the sidewalk. She glanced over her shoulder and saw him drive around the corner.

She crossed the street and cut down an alley. She heard braking tires. She climbed a fence and ran into a backyard. She stopped. She couldn't run anymore. Her heart was pounding. She could hardly breath. She spotted a large bush. She crawled underneath it, rolled into a small ball and silently prayed, *Please, God, please don't let him find me.*

She tried to breathe quietly, but the running had triggered her asthma. Every time she inhaled, she wheezed. Every time she exhaled, she squeaked. If he came near, he would hear her.

The gate opened. He walked into the yard, stopped and listened. She held her breath until she thought she would explode. He turned to leave. She had to take a breath. She wheezed, and he turned. He walked straight to the bush and pulled her out of her hiding place.

"You will never leave me," he snarled and began to strangle her.

She fought him, but it did no good. He was too strong. She felt herself getting weak. She was having trouble breathing. It was getting dark. *Oh,* she thought, *dark is nice. It doesn't hurt. I like the dark.* She quit struggling and passed out.

When Tamara awoke it was still dark. She was laying on the grass by the bush. Dale was gone. She had no idea how long she had been lying there. There was no rational time line for a night as insane as this one. She arose slowly and found her way home.

At home, she crawled into bed with her clothes on. She slept until noon and was shocked when she finally looked into the mirror. She did not recognize the swollen, bruised face reflected there. She took a long shower and crawled back into bed. Her face throbbed. Her neck was sore. Every muscle in her body hurt from stress and fear, but she managed to fall back into an exhausted sleep. A ringing phone interrupted her fitful slumber. She answered it and heard his voice.

"Tamara, is that you? Thank God, you are okay. I thought you were dead. I thought I had killed you. I am so sorry. It was the booze. You know I would never hurt you. I won't drink anymore. I love you."

"If you come near me, I'll report you to the police," she asserted, as she slammed down the phone.

As she sat down, she realized how much her body hurt. She closed her eyes and listened to the gentle wind rustling the trees. There were birds singing. The sun was filtering into the room. She realized how sore her heart was. *How did I get into this mess?* she asked herself. *Why did I ignore the warning signs?* Tamara knew the answer. She wanted desperately to be loved. Once again, she heard the loud ring of the phone.

"Don't hang up on me," he pleaded. "I promise, I'll never hurt you again."

"You got that right."

This time she unplugged the phone from the wall. *Never again,* she promised herself. *Never again will I let someone hurt me. Never again will I trade myself for love. Never!! I'd rather be alone. I'd rather go down fighting.*

Tamara told no one what had transpired that night. She blamed her bruises on a car accident. Kay was angry that she wouldn't answer Dale's calls or see him. Once or twice, Tamara found herself wanting to confide in her sister or her friends what had happened between her and Dale, but she was too embarrassed. She didn't want anyone to know she had been such a fool.

Tamara took a job as a waitress in another state immediately after graduation. Her mother forwarded a few letters from Dale. She set them, unopened, on the bureau in her apartment to remind her not to trust, not to love.

In the fall, Tamara returned to her home state to begin college, confident that she had totally put Dale behind her. She never saw Dale again, although he did haunt her dreams. She awoke many nights in a cold sweat, certain that he was carrying her into the dark over his shoulder. In all her nightmares, she had no legs.

Dale—The Stalker

Their paths did indirectly cross one more time. Several years after beginning college, Tamara had moved to a city three hours from her hometown. She was attending a university and competing in speech. Her favorite events were oratory and oral interpretation. She won many oratory contests, but never took first in oral interpretation because she was not as good as Rosie. Rosie was the best interper in the Northwest. Rosie was very attractive and possessed a passion and sweetness that won over audiences and judges.

Rosie attended college in the town where Tamara had grown up. Even though they were at different schools, Rosie and Tamara became good friends. Tamara looked forward to the opportunity to visit with Rosie at speech meets and discuss the people and places in her hometown.

After Christmas break of her third year of college, Tamara was competing in an out-of-state speech meet. It was a tough tournament, with top-notch competition. Everything was up for grabs, except interp. Everybody knew Rosie would win. Then, word got out that Rosie might not make the finals. She had new material, and it wasn't going over well with the judges. Tamara was glad Rosie was in her final preliminary round, so she could judge the new material for herself.

Rosie stepped to the front of the room with the quiet elegance that was her trademark. "I am going to read love poems," she announced with a sweet smile. But, when she started reading there was an obvious dichotomy between the romantic, passionate words and her strained, cynical tone.

After the round, Rosie and Tamara found an empty table in the campus coffee shop.

"What's wrong Rosie? You read those love poems with anger and fear."

"I'm engaged," Rosie answered evasively.

"Are congratulations in order?"

"No."

Rosie began to cry softly. Finally, she lifted her head, and looked at Tamara.

"He terrifies me. I don't want to marry him. I don't even want to date him. I tried to break up with him before Christmas. He was getting so possessive that it scared me. Christmas Eve he begged me to see him one last time, so he could give me my Christmas gift. He said he couldn't return it, so it could be a 'goodbye gift.' He can be really sweet when he wants to be. On our first date he took me to a park and kissed me on the swings."

"Oh, no," whispered Tamara.

"What's wrong," asked Rosie.

"Nothing. Go on. So, you met with him Christmas Eve. What happened then?"

"He took me to the Rimrocks. Do you know where that is?"

"Oh, yeah," said Tamara with a sickening feeling in her stomach, "I know it well."

"He drove to the edge of the Rims and took out a box. It was wrapped in gold paper with a big red ribbon. He opened it and took out a gun. He held it to my head and said, 'Here is your gift, Rosie. I'm going to kill you. Then, I'm going to kill myself. If I can't have you, no one will.'"

Rosie looked up at Tamara with the wide eyes of a scared child.

"I've never even seen a gun. I was so frightened. He held it against my temple and said, 'Are you sure you want to break up with me?'"

"What did you say," asked Tamara in a hushed voice.

"I told him I didn't want to break up. It was all a mistake. He said he thought so and took the gun away from my head. But, he didn't put it away. He kept it in one hand, while he pulled a small box out of the glove compartment. He told me to open the box. It was an engagement ring—this ring."

Rosie held up her trembling hand for Tamara to see. Tamara took the long slender hand in hers and asked, "Is his name Dale?" Rosie's eyes grew large. "How did you know?"

Tamara told her about the night of terror she experienced at Dale's hands.

"You have to get away from him, Rosie. He's crazy. Drop out of college if you have to. Transfer to another school. Go stay with friends somewhere. Oh, Rosie, this man is dangerous."

They held each other and parted, each going to her separate hotel room. Rosie checked out of her hotel in the middle of the night. She left a letter for the coach saying she was leaving because she had the flu. The coach wasn't surprised. He figured when he saw her poor scores that she wasn't feeling well. Tamara took first place, but she knew it was an empty win.

At the next speech tournament Tamara heard that Rosie had dropped out of college. No one knew where she went. Everyone thought it was a shame. Tamara was relieved, for Rosie and for herself.

A murky piece was added to the window.

The Lesson

Poor Choices

People are in abusive situations because they are making poor choices.

This obviously doesn't apply to children and the severely handicapped who have no power over those who hurt them. But, adults, young and old, find themselves in abusive relationships at home and at work because they make the choice to trade security for safety.

There are people who deliberately hurt others. There are people who build themselves up by tearing others down. We cannot go through life suspecting that everyone is out to do us harm or we will become negative and cynical. We must, however, be cautious with our trust.

So, how do we know who can be trusted? The decision is not as difficult as we think. Our intuition tells us when a relationship or situation is dangerous. We always hear a warning voice, we just don't always listen. We listen, instead, to the voices of friends we want to impress or family we want to please. Sometimes we allow the warning voice to be drowned out by our need for financial and emotional security. I listened to the wrong voices in my crisis with Dale. I am not the only one who has done so. There are many people reading this book who have allowed themselves to be misused in personal and work relationships.

Relationships should not hurt. Marriage should not hurt. Friendship should not hurt. Jobs should not hurt. That isn't to say that marriage, friendships and jobs are always easy. There will be challenging, times. But, there is a difference between a situation that is challenging and one that is destructive.

Some of the most abusive people in our lives are family members. We are not compatible with people just because we are related. All of us know family members who are so negative and intolerable that we would not walk across a room to talk to them if we met at a party. And, yet, we choose to allow them to mistreat and belittle us because we happen to share the same gene pool.

Remember, the world is ready to accept our opinions of ourselves. After all, we know ourselves best. If we tell people they have a right to walk on us, they will walk on us.

I have known many parents who are surprised when their children mistreat them. Many of these people have allowed their partners to be abusive for years. Why are they shocked when the children copy those destructive behaviors? The children have merely learned the lessons that their parents have taught.

There are two kinds of relationships—positive and poisonous. Positive relationships build us up. They are with people who appreciate us at our best and accept us at our worst. They are with people who allow us to be imperfect, but don't allow us to be destructive toward ourselves and others.

Poisonous relationships destroy us. They hurt. Sometimes poisonous relationships are obvious, such as those that pull us into the dangerous world of addiction and sexual compromise. But, more often, poisonous relationships are subtle in the way they hurt us. These relationships are with people who consume our positive energy and never replenish it. These relationships slowly destroy our self-esteem.

These are some of the warning signs that a relationship has become poisonous:

- We feel worse about ourselves when we spend time with the person.

- We make excuses for their behaviors.

- We find ourselves justifying our behaviors and viewpoints.

- We feel that we deserve the bad things that come our way.

- We feel that the good things we experience are a fluke.

- We are grateful for any attention and affection they give us.

- We remain in these relationships out of a sense of guilt or fear.

If we find ourselves in a poisonous relationship, we must do the following:

- We must take action. If we find ourselves in abusive situations, we must get out immediately. It won't be easy to leave. It is always difficult to make a change in our personal or professional lives. Change isn't easy, but it is possible. It is our choice.

- We must listen to the voice of God. He will tell us when someone is bad for us. We must respect ourselves enough to heed the warning.

- We must show respect for ourselves by protecting ourselves. We have the right to be safe.

No one has a right to abuse another person physically, emotionally or verbally. Not a parent, not a child, not a friend, and not a fellow worker or boss. There is an old saying—"If you want your ship to sail through life, stop every now and then, and scrape off the barnacles." If you want to survive the challenges and pain that come with life, ask yourself, "Are there barnacles that I should scrape off my life?"

Chapter Seven
Found

Tamara felt as if she had lived two lives. In her first life, she was lost in a pinball machine, batted around, forever reacting to forces out of her control. Sometimes, she would make a right move, and the lights would shine brightly, the bells ring loudly. Most of the time, she was propelled into dark holes, empty chutes, only to find herself back at the start of the endless game. Then, she met Kelly.

In her second life, she was wrapped in a warm blanket of love and acceptance. It was like lying on the white sands of a tropical beach. There would be times when she was chilled by cool rain. There would be times when she was battered by strong waves. She would even be stung by nasty pests and blowing sand. She knew with certainty, however, that the sun would always reappear and hold her in its warmth.

Kelly

Tamara set her sights on Kelly the second day of her freshman year at college. She selected him because he was the best looking guy who didn't already have a steady girlfriend. He was a naive farm boy, who had no experience with girls. He never had a chance.

Kelly was in Tamara's first period French class. He washed breakfast dishes in the college cafeteria and would arrive only seconds before class started. Knowing this, Tamara arrived at class twenty minutes early and put her purse on the chair beside her so that by the time Kelly arrived, the only vacant seat was next to her. (Once they were engaged, she never made it to class on time again.)

Tamara had two years of high school French, so she offered to help Kelly study. She was pleased when he said yes, but she soon discovered he was so hopelessly shy that he would never ask her out, no matter how long she tutored him.

There was a dance planned for the weekend. Tamara asked Kelly if he was going and when he nodded *yes*, she said she would save a dance for him. He smiled but said nothing.

The night of the dance Tamara told her roommate, "If Kelly doesn't ask me to dance by ten o'clock, I am going to put the moves on his roommate instead. He isn't as cute as Kelly, but, heh, a bird in the hand . . . and all that." She flirted shamelessly with Kelly and kept one eye on her watch. She had all but given up when at nine fifty-five, he asked her to dance. It was the beginning.

Their relationship progressed quickly, and soon they were inseparable. She found him easy to talk to. Once, when she told Kelly that her parents were divorced and her childhood had been unstable, he said he felt lucky because he had only good memories of his childhood on the farm.

Kelly was not like anyone Tamara had dated. He was a gentleman. He was kind. He was secure. He treated her with respect. He was the kind of guy she had always avoided. She was on unfamiliar turf, and it scared her.

He gave her a rose when she made the college cheering squad. He gave her a card of encouragement when she had a dentist appointment. Whether she was acting in plays, competing in speech meets, or singing in the choir, he sat in the front row.

Tamara was falling in love with Kelly, and it frightened her. She, unconsciously, reverted back to her protective behavior (used successfully with previous boyfriends) of driving him off before she was too vulnerable.

Kelly refused to leave. She indulged her anger, and he offered kindness. She lied, and he forgave. She boldly displayed her worst qualities, and he focused on her best. She gave up on him, and he refused to give up on them. The more she pushed him away, the more he held her close.

The day before Thanksgiving she got a desperate call from her fifteen-year-old sister, Vallia.

"You have to come home," Vallia sobbed. "Mom and Dad just left together. They are going to get married again."

Kelly could tell Tamara was upset. He borrowed his roommate's car and drove her home. When they entered the living room, they found Vallia on the floor holding her little brothers, Shane and Pat. All three looked at Tamara, their eyes full of tears and panic.

"Dad came home and demanded to see Mom," Vallia explained.

"She didn't let him?" Tamara queried.

"Yes, she did. He was really nice. You know how depressed she's been since the divorce. All she does is cry. Anyway, he said he had something for her. Then, he went to the stereo and put on a record of Irish love songs."

"Oh, no," Tamara moaned, "Irish songs. Mom could never say no to Irish songs."

"I know," Vallia nodded and continued. " Next thing I know, Dad's on his knees begging forgiveness, and Mom is swearing undying love. They were holding each other and crying. Then, he proposed, and they left."

"Wouldn't it be good if they remarried?" Kelly asked, as he innocently looked at Tamara.

"Of course not," Shane explained, using words much too wise for his eleven years. "They are incompatible. The fighting will begin again, once the passion has vanished. It always does."

"Why would they get married again?" Pat whispered, his nine-year-old eyes brimming with tears.

They looked at Tamara. She did what she always did when there were no answers. She made them laugh.

"Maybe Mom is pregnant," Tamara announced.

"What?" they asked in unison.

"You know, they probably had to get married," Tamara laughed.

"Oh," squealed Vallia, "that's gross."

"Can't you see it? Grampa out in the car with a shotgun and Mom all big and pregnant."

She grabbed a pillow off the sofa and stuffed it under her shirt. It wasn't all that funny, but it was the best she could do under pressure, and it worked. They giggled. Shane had a quick wit and only needed to be prompted.

"Just think," he joked, "if Mom had twins, we could be the Van Trapp Family Singers."

"Not the Van Trapp Family," quipped Tamara, "the 'Shut your Trap' Family Singers."

The laughter momentarily diverted their pain.

"What do you say we go for pizza and a movie?" asked Tamara.

"How about the Sound of Music," giggled Vallia.

After the movie, they stayed up late playing Monopoly. The next day was Thanksgiving, and Tamara cooked her first turkey. She followed the cookbook instructions, and all went well. As everyone watched in anticipation, she lifted the golden bird from the oven. It was too heavy. She dropped it. The lid flew off the roaster, and the turkey slid the entire length of the kitchen floor, stopping only when it slammed into the opposite wall. Everyone gasped, waiting for angry shouts of reprimand. Then, they remembered there were no adults there to scold them, and they laughed until their sides hurt.

Later that night, when her younger siblings were asleep, Tamara confided in Kelly, "Shane is right you know. Mom and Dad are incompatible. It will all start again." Then, she allowed herself to do something she had not done for a very long time. She cried. Kelly held her very close and stroked her hair. It felt right.

Kelly went home to his farm in Idaho for Christmas, and Tamara went with her family on a skiing trip. Her parents argued the entire vacation.

One afternoon, Tamara heard someone calling her name from across the ski chalet. She saw Jim, an old boyfriend, waving at her. After they visited for a few minutes, he asked, "I'm having a New Year's Eve party tomorrow night. Can you come?" Tamara accepted without hesitation. She wanted to be as far from her parents as possible because New Year's Eve undoubtedly meant drinking—and, drinking meant war.

She went to the party and lost herself in the laughter, drinking, and dancing. At midnight, loud voices were counting down from ten, and everyone was shouting, "Happy New Year!" Jim put his arm around her neck and kissed her. Tamara started to respond and, then, memories of Kelly's smile flooded her heart. She pushed Jim away, grabbed a glass of champagne and left the house.

She walked into the woods alone. The moon was bright. There was no sound except the fresh snow crunching under her footsteps. She sat on a large boulder, sipped the champagne and lost herself in the quiet.

Tamara was at a crossroads. She loved Kelly, but she was terrified of commitment. What if she gave her heart and he left her? What if they ended up like her parents—unable to live with each other, unable to live without each other? She was afraid and confused. For the first time since she started the hectic life of a college student, she closed her eyes and prayed out loud.

"Tell me, God. is he the right one?"

"Yes, he is the right one," a voice answered.

The voice startled her. She opened her eyes and looked around. She was alone. She closed her eyes and listened to the stillness.

On New Year's Eve, 1968, Tamara heard the voice of God say, "My child, all those nights you cried in the dark, I listened. All the times you pleaded to be loved, I heard. I have sent Kelly for you. He is the answer to your prayers. And, Tamara . . .."

"Yes, God."

"Don't blow this!"

One month later, Kelly sat nervously in Tamara's family's living room.

"May I marry your daughter?" he asked Kay.

"She is only eighteen, and you are only twenty. How do you expect to support her?"

"I have $500.00 in savings, a motorcycle, and a milk cow," Kelly replied earnestly.

Kay started to giggle.

"Stop laughing," snapped Tamara.

"You can't be serious. A milk cow!"

Kay's giggle's became all-out hysterics. Tamara and Kelly stomped angrily out of the room.

They were married on June 1, 1968.

Years later, when Tamara and Kelly were blessed with daughters of their own, they would be more understanding of Kay's reaction. After all, they were young and had little visible means of support. However, they never missed the opportunity to remind Kay that Kelly's monthly milk check paid the rent for their married student housing, and when they earned their degrees, they sold the cow to cover the doctor bills for their second child.

Tamara approached marriage with the same stubborn conviction she did everything else. Whenever challenges threatened their commitment to each other, Tamara would recall the voice of God reassuring her on a clear night, high in the mountains of Montana, "He is the answer to your prayers. Don't blow this."

An integral piece of glass was added to the window, giving clarity and security to the other pieces.

The Lesson

To be Loved

Kelly taught me I could be accepted and loved–the greatest gift one person can give another. It was not easy for me to accept the gift. It was difficult for me to trust Kelly because trust meant being vulnerable, but relationships cannot survive without trust.

When Kelly and I had been married five years, we volunteered to talk to a high school home economics class about relationships. Kelly was so overwhelmed with stage fright that he answered all questions with a simple, "Yes" or "No."

"What would you do if Kelly cheated on you?" a girl asked Tamara.

"He wouldn't."

"Yeah, but, what if he did?" she repeated.

"He wouldn't," I insisted.

"That's no answer," challenged the student.

"Yes, it is," Kelly interrupted.

Every student stared at him. His conviction gave him the courage to continue.

"I took a wedding vow to love my wife and be faithful, and that is what I intend to do."

"What if things change? What if she changes?" asked one boy.

"It doesn't matter," Kelly said firmly. "A vow is a vow. Things may change, but my promise is forever."

"But," one girl asserted, "what if you meet someone you love more? Would you deny those feelings."

"Absolutely," Kelly persisted. "Marriage isn't about feelings. It is about commitment. I said 'until death do us part,' and I meant it."

Kelly was right. Marriage isn't about feelings. It is about commitment. I am a true romantic. I love candles in the bedroom, roses in winter, and happy endings, but I know the commitment of marriage goes beyond romance.

Marriage requires sacrifice. It only works when those involved are willing to look beyond their own needs and focus on those they love. Couples must accept each other, warts and all. There are no perfect relationships because there are no perfect people.

There are far too many couples who are not willing to honor that sacrifice. Surveys show that today's young people are cynical about relationships. Who can blame them? They have been well trained by my generation.

Unlike generations before, baby boomers view marriage as a semi-serious responsibility and divorce as an ever-present escape hatch. Baby boomers have left a social legacy of disrespect about the sanctity of marriage.

Let me make it perfectly clear; I am not criticizing those who have walked away from physically, verbally, or emotionally abusive marriages. Love should not hurt. Healthy people divorce themselves from abusive relationships.

But, far too many couples are searching for high-return, low-risk relationships that exist only in fairy tales and Hollywood movies. They expect marriage to be an emotional and physical panacea consisting of job security, fancy homes, perfect kids, congenial in-laws and, of course, great sex.

Marriage may include these elements, but it is just as likely to include job lay-offs, high mortgages, rebellious kids, demanding in-laws, and times when fatigue replaces passion. Even if life is miraculously uncomplicated, the couple will still go through change. They will gain weight, lose their hair, experience illness, and reshape their values and goals. They will grow up and grow old, but they do not have to grow apart. They can choose to stand together through the tough times and grow together through the bad times.

It is also important to remember that divorce is difficult. Divorce hurts. It hurts everyone involved, especially the children. And, subsequent marriages usually paint new faces on the same old problems. People recover from the pain of divorce and go on because they have no other choice. It makes more sense for couples to agree that building a strong marriage is a better choice.

My heart goes out to those who have experienced the emotional, economical and physical trauma of divorce. They need our support. Single parenting is an exhausting challenge. Those who have gone through the trauma of divorce owe it to themselves to learn from the situation and not repeat their mistakes. Those who are still married must tenaciously fight for their marriage.

People often tell me, "You and Kelly are so lucky to be happily married." I am blessed, but luck has nothing to do with it. It starts with the decision that marriage vows are forever. It requires making the time to know each other and taking the time to enjoy each other. Most importantly, it demands a sense of humor and a whole lot of help from God. Marriage isn't for those who are emotionally lazy or naively romantic.

Far too many couples today have embraced compromising situations in the name of passion and romance. There is nothing romantic about hurting the people you love.

Marriage is a wild roller coaster ride of highs and lows, but if two people choose to honor their marriage vows, they will discover the rewards are immeasurable. They will grow old with their best friend, and it doesn't get any better than that.

PART TWO

Survival Lessons—
Stepping Forward

Chapter Eight
Learning From Tera

1970

can do this. I can do this." Then, another wave of all encompassing pain.

"I can't do this. I can't do this. Someone make it stop, please."

I had been in labor for over thirty-five hours. I was twenty. I was scared. I was drowning.

"Oh God," I whispered, "How did I get into this?"

1968

Kelly and I drove to Denver for our honeymoon. We chose Denver because they had an awesome amusement park and served 3.2 beer to eighteen-year olds. Those reasons reconfirmed for our parents that we were much too immature to be getting married. Kelly departed immediately after our honeymoon for basic training in Pensacola, Florida.

The previous year, Kelly had received a letter declaring him the proud recipient of a low draft number. With that one piece of mail, the Viet Nam war had ceased being a remote occurrence on the evening news. Kelly was a college freshman.

He spent a sleepless night examining his options and, the next day, walked into the Naval recruiting office with a determination to control his own destiny. He walked out a member of the Aviation Officer Candidate program. The Navy gave him no financial assistance, but did agree to let him finish college. During summer breaks, Kelly would attend basic training in Pensacola, Florida, and immediately after graduation, he would be commissioned an officer and attend flight school. He would also owe the Navy six years of dedicated service.

Kelly told me of his commitment to the Navy shortly after we started dating, but we seldom discussed it. We were too busy planning for our future to worry about war.

I spent the first three months of our married life at the Hall's farm in Idaho with Kelly's wonderful parents, while he marched, slept and trained in the heat and humidity of Florida. I missed him terribly. Sometimes, the evening news would show the bombs and bodies of the war; I would become consumed with fear. But, Kelly would easily mollify my worries during our phone conversations. "I have two and a half years of college left," he would say with confidence. "Viet Nam won't last two more years."

When Kelly returned in the fall, we transferred to Montana State University because it was less expensive. We moved to married student housing with everything we owned in the back of a borrowed pick-up. We unpacked used furniture, a stained carpet we found discarded in the trash and boxes of silver and crystal wedding gifts. I entered marriage with a stack of Beatle records, the determination to be a good wife and the desire to have a child as soon as possible.

Kelly and I had been married eleven months when I announced that we should have a child. We were full-time college students working at a variety of minimum wage jobs. The timing was less than ideal, but we were too young to notice. I was ready for a change; married life was getting routine. My reasons were weak, but my determination was strong.

1969

I learned 2 weeks after our first wedding anniversary that I was pregnant. Kelly was in Pensacola for his second summer of Naval training. I sent him a telegram that read "Congratulations. There is a new plane in the hanger." That night, he got drunk with his navy buddies. Before he passed out on the beach, he gazed at the stars and asked God to help him be a good father.

The discovery that I was pregnant filled me with a contradiction of emotions–joy and fear. I had wanted a baby to love since I was nine and had held my newborn brother, Patrick, in my arms. Patrick was adorable, vulnerable and trusting; he was perfect in every way. I vowed that I would let no harm come to him. It was a vow born out of love and naivete. Unfortunately, when I was nineteen my perception of motherhood was still just as naive. I thought babies were perfect, and loving mothers competent.

The thought of being pregnant thrilled me. The thought of giving birth terrified me. I left the doctor's office with stacks of pamphlets and checked books out of the college library. The literature agreed on one point: it was dangerous to take pain medication. It was advised that mothers stay calm in labor and breathe deeply. *How asinine*, I thought. At my next checkup, I told the doctor that breathing deeply sounded more like a placebo than an antidote for pain.

I said, (only half jokingly), "I prefer the system they used when my mother had babies."

"And, what system was that?" he asked.

"The doctor knocked her out with drugs the minute labor started and woke her up when her kids were entering kindergarten."

"Oh, no, Tamara," he responded, much too seriously, "a drug-free birth is much better for the baby and the mother."

I wasn't convinced, but I wanted to do what was right for my baby, so I practiced breathing.

The hospital offered a one-hour prenatal class for expectant parents. The nurse told us the preliminary stages of labor lasted only eight to ten hours. She assured us that once we were wheeled from the labor room to the delivery room, we would be in the final stage of labor.

"Bearing down is the worst part of the birth, but it lasts only fifteen to thirty minutes. Anyone can withstand thirty minutes of pain if she puts her mind to it," the nurse insisted.

Then, we viewed a movie of a staged delivery. The perfectly coiffed mother did not smear her make-up or break into a sweat. The movie ended with her holding a perfect baby in her arms and cooing jubilantly to her proud husband, "Oh honey, labor wasn't that bad. I'm so glad I didn't ask for pain medicine."

One of my books suggested that the mother-to-be could prepare for labor by laying quietly in a dark room, recalling her worst menstrual cramps and then visualizing herself conquering the pain. I fell asleep every night breathing deeply, visualizing myself conquering menstrual cramps and whispering, "Anyone can withstand thirty minutes of pain." I was sure I was ready for labor. I was wrong.

1970

Nothing had prepared me for the intensity or length of pain that could be involved in having a baby. By the time I went to the hospital, I had been in labor eighteen hours. I screamed at the nurses, swore at God and struck at Kelly when he suggested I calm down and breathe deeply. The poor man stared at me with shock wondering when I would turn into the smiling woman he saw in the training video.

I begged for something to stop the pain. The doctor prescribed hand-held canisters of gas. I was told to inhale when each pain reached its climax. Seven gas canisters later, the doctor said it was time for me to be wheeled into the delivery room. I had been in labor thirty-two hours.

I was holding onto sanity by a thread. The thread snapped when the head nurse told Kelly he could not accompany me into the delivery. I clutched his hand and begged the nurse to change her mind.

"Absolutely not. The last thing I need is a father passing out during delivery."

"I won't pass out," asserted Kelly. "I grew up on a farm. I have pulled calves out of cows with ropes."

"I can assure you," she snorted, "this isn't a farm, and we don't use ropes."

"I feel like a cow," I yelled, "and if ropes would help get this baby out–use them!"

The nurse gave me a look of disdain and demanded that Kelly go to the waiting room.

"We'll let you know when it's over," she told him.

She wheeled me towards the delivery room. A new pain encompassed me. I shrieked.

"Stop screaming," the nurse growled. "For Pete's sake, you aren't the only woman who has had a baby. It isn't that bad."

"How many hours were you in labor?" I charged.

"I've never had a baby, but I've delivered plenty."

"That doesn't count," I responded sarcastically. "I've eaten chicken but that doesn't mean I know what it feels like to push an egg out my butt."

"Don't be gross," she snapped. She pushed my bed toward the delivery room nurse and said, "Good luck with this one. She's impossible."

"What's new," I said as another wave of pain attacked.

I squeezed my eyes shut and focused on the reassuring words I had heard in the prenatal class: "When you get to the delivery room you will have only thirty minutes of labor left. Anyone who puts her mind to it can withstand thirty minutes of pain."

Four hours later, the doctor resorted to using forceps to free my baby. I was delirious from exhaustion and pain.

"You have a daughter," the doctor said in a strained voice.

"Is she okay?," I whispered, hoarse from screaming.

There was silence. I realized I had not heard my baby cry.

"We think so," the doctor said softly. "It was a long delivery. I would have warned you if I had known it was going to be so difficult."

"If I'd known it was going to be so difficult, I wouldn't have gotten pregnant!" I murmured.

And then they placed my precious daughter Tera in my arms, and all the pain was forgotten.

I stared at her face. My eyes immediately focused on quarter size, scarlet marks on each side of her forehead.

"What are these marks?" I asked, panic rising in my voice.

"They are nothing to be concerned about," responded the doctor. "They are normal in forcep deliveries. They will disappear within hours."

I held her close and fell asleep, overwhelmed with love.

Later that afternoon, I studied every inch of her tiny being. She had long, soft eyelashes, a delicate nose and a tulip-shaped mouth. I counted her fingers. Ten. I unwrapped the blanket and counted her toes. Ten.

"You are perfect in every way, just like I knew you would be," I whispered.

I was wrong.

I started to nurse her and she twitched. It was a short, intense twitch, like a jerking. It scared me. I called the nurse.

"Quick movements are normal," the nurse reassured. "All babies react to their new environment."

The next day I was concerned because the marks on her temples were not fading. Every time I held her against my shoulder and patted her back, I could smell the gas from the canisters on her breath. Once again, I rang the nurse.

"Everything is normal. The only thing wrong with her is a nervous mother," she laughed.

I tried to take consolation in the nurse's comments, but a little voice inside said, "Something IS wrong." Sadly, it would be years before I would learn to trust that voice.

Tera's jerking did not stop. Finally, the intense twitching was observed by the nurse, who called the doctor. He examined Tera in the nursery. Later, the doctor told Kelly and me that Tera had epilepsy and would probably be retarded.

"Was it the gas?" I asked.

"Of course not," insisted the doctor, "these things just happen."

I didn't believe him. Guilt and worry swallowed my joy.

"I'm sorry for hurting you," I whispered to my defenseless child.

I was in shock. I was twenty years old and the first mentally disabled person I laid eyes on was my own daughter. I had attended dozens of schools in two states and one Canadian Province and there hadn't been any handicapped kids in those schools. I didn't know where physically and mentally handicapped people lived. Everything in society was geared for "normal" people. For the first time in my life, I wondered what happened to those who weren't normal.

1971

Kelly graduated from college and we drove from Montana to Pensacola in a dilapidated old Chevy with Tera in a playpen in the back seat. Tera was hospitalized twice in Florida for seizures. The military hospital, with its rigid visiting hours and sterile environment, made us appreciate the hospital back home. The Navy doctor told us to delete "epilepsy" from Tera's records, or she would be banned from attending Florida schools.

Kelly was an excellent soldier. He had been voted one of the top two candidates by his fellow classmates and supervisors. Kelly quickly discovered, however, that he suffered from severe motion sickness. He was seriously wondering how he would be able to fly a jet with his head in a barf bag. The flight program was voluntary, but if he quit he would undoubtedly be shipped to Viet Nam. Just when things seemed impossible, we received the best possible news.

The Navy announced they had recruited too many students into the flight program. They offered "early outs" to those who wished to discontinue the flight program IF the Navy thought their college degrees were not compatible with other Navy assignments. Kelly's degree in agriculture was a clear winner. We returned to Montana. One year later, there was an escalation in the war, and the Navy, once again, increased their recruiting efforts. The controversial war in a strange country was taking the lives of people we knew, and we were suddenly aware of how lucky we had been.

1972

The months were a blur of drugs, seizures and hospital visits. The doctor prescribed phenobarbital. The seizures continued. He prescribed more. Tera became so hyperactive she couldn't sleep. I suggested the medicine was making her worse. The doctor said I was a nervous mother. That voice inside said he was wrong, but I disregarded the voice because he was the doctor and I was just the mother. When Tera had over thirty seizures in one twenty-four hour period, the doctor decided the phenobarbital was making her worse.

He switched her to three strong anticonvulsants. Over the next six months, Tera went from a hyperactive child who ran everywhere to a zombie who slept twenty hours a day and crawled lethargically around the apartment. I called the doctor's office constantly. The nurse told me I was a nervous mother. Once again, a voice told me I was right. Once again, I didn't trust myself.

On her second birthday, I dressed Tera in a new birthday dress, curled her hair and sat her in front of a big chocolate cake for pictures. She was too weak to sit up. She fell face first into the cake. I marched to the phone and called the doctor's office.

"You tell the doctor there is something seriously wrong with my daughter. I am bringing her in right now," I screamed, slamming down the phone.

"I promise I will make the doctor listen to me," I whispered to Tera as I strapped her into her car seat. In order to build up my confidence, I rehearsed my angry speech out loud as I drove to his office. I never delivered that speech.

The doctor entered the room. Tera stood and struggled to walk towards me. She stumbled, as if drunk. She was weak and disoriented. Her large eyes were dazed. She could not focus.

"I want you to take her to the Denver Children's Hospital immediately", the doctor said.

Tera and I flew to Denver. Tests revealed toxic levels of medications in her blood. She was a very sick little girl, but the other children were sicker. I walked the halls, observing helpless children fighting horrid diseases and debilitating birth defects. I cried with mothers younger than me, as we watched brave babies endure agonizing treatments that would prolong life, but not save it. I had thrown my college textbooks into the suitcase, intending to do homework while Tera was sleeping. Those intentions did not become a reality. Each passing day made book reports and English essays seem trivial.

I was grateful I wasn't alone. My mother had remarried the previous winter and moved to Denver. Her new husband, Harry, was a kind man who had welcomed into his heart my little brothers Shane and Patrick. Harry was retired and financially secure. He paid for my airline ticket. He drove me to the hospital everyday and sat quietly reading a book in the waiting room. His warm eyes gave me comfort and his gentle ways reminded me of my Kelly, whom I missed terribly.

Tera improved steadily and ten days later she was released. The neurologist told me there was no way to know how much permanent damage Tera had suffered due to the overdose of medication. She told me to find a new doctor when I got home and to bring Tera back at least once a year for a checkup.

I thanked the doctor and asked her to sign an absenteeism slip verifying to the university Dean of Students that I had an acceptable excuse for missing class. She shook her head and said as she signed her name, "Well, this is one for the record book."

The day we left the hospital, I agreed to a payment schedule for the hospital bills.

1973

One month before I graduated from college, I had my second child. The delivery was a surprisingly short twelve hours. I took Lemaze classes and my screams could barely be heard outside of the hospital. Tiffani had a delightful disposition and was appropriately nicknamed Sunshine because she smiled constantly, unless someone teased Tera. Tiffani's gentle mood would change dramatically. She would become her sister's staunch protector.

1974

Tera's disability was only obvious when she spoke because her speech was slow and hesitant. Regularly she would be hospitalized for seizures. Injections would stop the cycle, and we would take her home to recover. I would lay her on a mattress in the living room so she didn't feel isolated. I would diaper and feed her until her strength and coordination returned. Usually the lethargic state caused by the seizures and drugs would last a week, then she would be back running and playing with other kids.

1975

When Tera was five and Tiffani eighteen months old, Troy was born. We nicknamed him Trooper. He was a moving turbo of energy who challenged every rule and melted my heart with his giggle. He sucked the fourth finger of his right hand until the kids on the school bus teased him. He had a gentle heart. When he was three, he sat quietly on the floor listening to Barbra Streisand sing, "You Don't Send Me Flowers." He turned to me with a serious look and said, "That lady sounds sad. Can she come live with us?"

1976

Tera was trying to put on her socks. Her little fingers were struggling. The look of determination in her eyes quickly turned to anger.

"You can do it, Tera," I encouraged.

My words were interrupted by a wail from Troy. I rushed to answer his needs. Tera's frustration reached its boiling point. Her loud screams joined Troy's in an ear-splitting cacophony. Three-year-old Tiffani pulled at my leg and said, "I can help, Mommy. Should I put Tera's socks on?"

I looked at Tiffani's innocent face and realized I didn't know the answer to her question. I didn't know if Tera needed help. That was the never-ending struggle of raising a special child. "How much help should I give?" If I did too much for Tera, she would be dependent on me. If I did too little, she would be frustrated. If I expected too much, it would be cruel. If I expected too little, it would be damaging.

Tera was wailing, "I can't. I can't." Troy was screeching. Tiffani was pleading, "Should I help Tera? Should I, Mom? Should I?"

I was overwhelmed with helplessness. I cried out in confusion, "God, please tell me whether Tera can put her socks on." I did not receive a clear answer.

1977–1981

Tera enthusiastically entered school, and I enthusiastically entered the battle for the rights of the handicapped. I sat on committees and demanded equal opportunity for my daughter. Kelly started an apprenticeship program to become a plumber. I worked part-time as a substitute teacher and speech coach. Then, I taught at the University. All three children were active in music, 4-H, sports and church. I fell back into my favorite escape mechanism of staying too busy to think about the challenges of life. I served on the school board and took college classes. I ran from sun-up until sun-down and fell into bed convinced that my exhaustion meant everything was under control.

1982

Our home fell apart.

The intensity and frequency of Tera's temper tantrums increased. She screamed, hit, bit and threw things. Each day, she encountered a new skill that came easily for her sister and brother, yet frustrated her: riding a bike, reading a book, writing a letter. She was constantly angry.

142

Tiffani developed migraines. Trooper developed hostility. Kelly avoided the stress by putting in long hours at work or outside on our ten acres. It was only a matter of time until someone cracked under the pressure. It was me.

It was a typical morning. Tera was verbally and physically aggressive. I was curling her hair for the Christmas program.

"Don't burn me," she cried.

"I won't burn you," I reassured.

"Don't, don't," she yelled, swinging her arms wildly.

"Fine, I won't curl your hair."

I slammed down the curling iron and turned to leave the room. She screamed. I walked back. She swung at me. I walked away. She screamed and kicked. I walked back. She threw the brush at me. I was so frustrated, I was shaking.

"Curl my hair. Curl my hair," she demanded.

Once again, I approached. Once again, she hit me.

"I'm through," I snapped, unplugging the curling iron and throwing it into the drawer.

"Curl my hair, curl my hair." Her screams were deafening.

"No," I shouted. "I'm not going to curl your hair."

Tera jumped up and clawed at my face. I covered myself with my arms and dodged her blows. I felt anger and frustration overtaking me. I shoved her backwards out of the bathroom and slammed the door. I heard a loud crashing sound and a scream. I quickly opened the door and saw her sitting on the floor. The intensity of her yelling revealed more anger than pain. She had obviously fallen from the force of my shove. She was shrieking, "Mommy hurt me. Mommy hurt me."

Tiffani came running into the hallway, looked at me with frightened, accusing eyes and asked, "Why did you hurt Tera?"

"I didn't hurt Tera. She fell," I explained loudly.

It was a bizarre scene: Twelve-year-old Tera, sitting on the floor, throwing the temper tantrum of a two-year-old. Seven-year-old Trooper eating his breakfast and refusing to acknowledge the pandemonium. Nine-year-old Tiffani, with her hands on her hips, demanding an explanation. A thirty-three-year-old mother, justifying herself while her husband sat in the barn oblivious to everything.

After the children left for the school bus, I sat on the couch and cried. I knew I hadn't hurt Tera, but I knew I could have. I had been out of control. I shivered just thinking about it. *Oh, God,* I thought, *I'm becoming my parents.* No one knew better than I the devastation of being physically mistreated as a child. Twenty years before, I had promised myself that I would someday have my own children and they would know only love and protection.

"No one will ever hurt my child," I had vowed before God. I had broken that vow. The pain and guilt were paralyzing. When the children climbed off the school bus seven hours later, I was still lying on the couch.

Later that night, when the children were in bed, Kelly and I had the first serious argument of our fourteen-year marriage.

"We need help. We can't handle Tera," I told Kelly.

"I don't think things are that bad," Kelly said softly.

"I almost hit her today."

"But, you didn't."

"Next time I might."

"You wouldn't do that. It's going to be okay."

"Stop it," I yelled. "Stop pretending everything is okay. I know you, Kelly. You don't want to be the bad guy. Well, fine, I'll be the bad guy. I'm used to it. I cannot handle Tera. There, I said it. I cannot handle Tera. I need help. Don't you understand? I am going to hit her, and I refuse to go to jail for child abuse just so you can pretend everything is fine."

Tears were streaming down my face. I began to shake. Kelly reached out his arm to console me. I pushed his arm away and turned to leave the bedroom.

"Don't be mad at me," Kelly pleaded.

"I am mad at you. I hate you."

"Why?" Kelly asked with shock in his eyes.

"Because I never wanted to make you choose between me and Tera. I hate you because you would let this family be destroyed before you would choose. So, now I am making you. Either Tera leaves, or I leave."

I slammed the bedroom door. I walked into the living room and stood gazing at the Christmas tree. The tinsel hung in uneven, waist-high clumps where they had been strewn by the hands of children. Brightly wrapped packages waited for that moment when squeals would cry, "It's just what I wanted." The glow of crackling embers in the fireplace outlined empty felt stockings hung on the mantel. I had spent hours carefully constructing those stockings from memories of the ones my mother had made for my brothers, sister and me. Next to the fireplace, sat the twelve-year-old rocking chair that had been my first-ever Mother's Day present.

"What kind of mother am I, God?"

I sank onto the floor and pulled my knees to my chest. In the shadows of the blinking Christmas lights, I revisited the despair, doubt and guilt I had known so well as a child.

Then I felt the warmth of Kelly's strong arms around my shoulders.

"I am so sorry, Tam," Kelly lifted my face in his hands and looked softly into my eyes, "you didn't make me choose between you and Tera. You just made me admit I need help. I am a stubborn German farmer. I hate asking for help."

"I'm a stubborn Italian, Irishwoman. I don't ask," I smiled. "I yell."

"I don't want to be a failure as a father."

"You will never be a failure as a father."

We held each other all night long under the Christmas tree.

Answers

We sent Tera back to the Denver Children's Hospital for an intense, one-month, residential evaluation program. For the first time in twelve years, we had answers. We learned that she was angry because her brain damage was much like that of a stroke victim. She comprehended twice as much as she could output. Her academic level was that of a first grader and her social skills a few years higher. She possessed a high understanding of relationships. She knew that people treated her differently than others and that awareness created understandable pain and frustration for her. The neurologist ended by saying, "We strongly recommend that Tera be placed in a residential treatment program that offers behavioral modification and medical supervision."

"You mean move her outside of our home?" I asked in a startled voice. "Did we do something wrong?"

"Not at all," the neurologist smiled. "Tera is one of the most demanding children we have evaluated. The staff member that was assigned to her was exhausted by the end of an eight-hour shift. Frankly, we are amazed that you have been able to keep her home for so long."

"But, it wouldn't be right to send her away," I protested.

"Let me be clear with you," the doctor continued. "Tera can be a delightful child, but she can also be violent. If she doesn't receive intensive behavioral modification and medical treatment, she is going to be a threat to herself and to others."

New Beginning

We found an excellent program for Tera. It was expensive, but our savings covered the cost. The home and school program offered consistent expectancies and reinforcement. Kelly and I realized after Tera left just how much energy and time she had consumed. We were shocked to discover we did not really know Tiffani and Trooper. They had been in Tera's shadow, receiving scraps of emotion and attention. Kelly and I thoroughly enjoyed discovering what delightful, unique children they were.

Tera was gone for eighteen months. We visited her often and she came home for holidays. Tiffani lost her migraines and Trooper found his smile. Kelly and I rediscovered the peace of companionship. Life was still challenging, but it was manageable.

In my head, I knew we were doing the right thing. But at night, I had nightmares of FCJ, and I awoke with the horrible fear that I had abandoned my child.

Tera came home, and we worked as a family to preserve the new behaviors she had learned. It was an on-going challenge because ours was an active household, and we could not provide the rigid consistency that made her time away so positive.

Tera had a fulfilling high school career. She received vocational training. She went to prom with another mentally disabled boy. They danced every dance, and she woke up the next day and announced, "My feet tingle from dancing all night."

I smiled and thought to myself, *Thank you, God, that Tera wasn't born in the "Good Old Days" when special kids weren't allowed in school.*

Tera competed in Special Olympics. She lit the torch in front of 3,000 people at the state games and the smile on her face shown brighter than the torch.

She graduated with her class when she was nineteen. Her diploma looked like everyone else's on the outside. Inside, it was a special education diploma. And, when they announced her name and she walked across the stage, the graduates in her class cheered louder than they had for the athletes or the scholars or the musicians. They cheered for the kid who did the most with what she had. I got to give Tera her diploma because I was on the school board. I cried openly. I was proud of her and proud of her classmates for acknowledging the joy of diversity.

Today Tera lives in a group home in our hometown and works at an employment center for the mentally challenged. It is a fulfilling life. It is a challenging life. Monitoring her medications is an ongoing battle. When her levels are too high she is lethargic, when they are too low, she is violent. Like all adults, she struggles with relationships. She adores her brother and sister. Their accomplishments are now a source of joy for her rather than a source of frustration.

She spends Sundays and holidays with us. She has a strong bond with God and gets very upset if she misses church. She calls every Saturday and reminds us to pick her up in the morning for bread and wine. Kelly once joked, "It's pretty humbling when the spiritual leader of our home is our mentally disabled daughter."

Last Easter the priest passed out paper. He asked us to draw a picture of God on one side. I handed Tera a pencil. She drew a cross and a heart. Then he asked us to write down, "Why does God love me?"

Tera cannot read or write, so she handed me the paper and asked me to write for her.

"Why does God love you?" I asked Tera.

A grin of innocence, that most of us sacrifice for adulthood, spread across her face.

"Silly Mom, He just does," she announced with certainty.

And a bright piece of the window was put into place

The Lesson:

Raising Tera was not an easy journey, but it is one I wouldn't have missed for the world. Granted, there were discouraging times when Kelly and I felt totally unequipped for the challenge. There were painful times when we were stung by the judgement of family and friends who did not understand the trials we faced. There were frustrating times when well-meaning (yet insensitive) people said, "God never gives you more than you can handle." We wanted to respond, "Yeah, well sometimes He misses it by a house." But when we look back, it is clear that God didn't make a mistake. Our house was the perfect home for Tera, and she was the perfect child for us. It was our goal to teach Tera love, acceptance and self reliance. In the end, she taught us more than we taught her. She made our lives richer and, in the process, taught the following lessons.

Don't Judge. Tera has taught us that it is wrong to let other people define our personal success. Everyday Tera struggles to perform skills that we take for granted. Skills like crossing a street or counting money. Her accomplishments, although minor in the eyes of many, illustrate courage and perseverance. Eleanor Roosevelt once said, "No one can make you feel inferior without your consent." Other people have no right to judge us because they do not live our lives or carry our burdens. They do not know where we started so they cannot evaluate where we are.

Love Unconditionally. Tera has taught us to love by modeling the acceptance and forgiveness of a child. Her voice squeals with excitement when I phone her. Her face lights up when I walk into the group home. I am humbled by the total acceptance she displays towards me. Tera is not capable of sarcasm, cynicism, or deceit. She never feels sorry for herself. She is forgiving towards the faults of others. She offers the trust of a child to anyone who is kind to her. Sadly, that trust makes her an easy target for those who would prey on the fragile and defenseless. Therefore, we must teach her the realities of our dangerous world. But every now and then, she joyously pulls us into her world. She leaves cookies for Santa Claus and carrots for the Easter bunny. She lets dogs lick her face and kittens climb in her lap. She believes the characters at Disney World are real and the Beatles who perform at Epcot are the actual Beatles. And, when a young man with long hair and a tidy dark beard served her communion one Sunday, she whispered in a voice filled with awe, "Jesus was at church today, and he gave me bread and wine."

Life isn't easy for Tera, but then life isn't easy for anyone. She lives a full life and, in many ways, is happier than any of us. Just once in my life, I would love to believe that Santa Claus was real, the Beatles were still together and Jesus served me communion.

All Children Are Challenging. In many ways, Kelly and I were luckier than other parents because we knew early on that it would be a challenge raising Tera. In reality, all children are a challenge. The only guarantee that accompanies babies is the guarantee that there will be heartache. Every child experiences mental, physical and emotional pain, and every parent, experiences their child's pain.

Does that mean we shouldn't have kids? Of course not. But, it does mean we should remove the rose-colored glasses. Otherwise, we are destined to be trapped in a pity party with *Why Me?* records playing in the background.

All Parents Make Mistakes. I made serious mistakes in parenting my children, but I refuse to feel guilty because I loved them with all my heart and I did my very best.

When my children were young I would start each morning with the earnest prayer, "God, I promise that today I will not lose my patience. Today, I will not get angry. Today, I will not get frustrated." And, God would smile and whisper, "Then you better stay in bed, because you are human and, therefore, fallible."

Parents who are afraid of making mistakes become so paralyzed with fear that they abdicate the responsibility of parenting. They usually raise spoiled, manipulative children who refuse to be accountable for their actions. The most difficult time our family faced was when Tera terrorized us with violent outbursts and selfish tantrums because Kelly and I were afraid to discipline her. Luckily, we learned from our mistake.

Parents must not be afraid to tell children when their behavior is unacceptable. Parents must not allow children to abuse themselves or others. Parents must not allow children to intimidate them with guilt. When Tiffani and Troy were rebellious teens, I hung a sign in the kitchen that said, "So it's not a perfect home. Adapt."

Disciplining children is easier and more effective if parents work together. Children are astute and instinctively know that the best formula for accomplishing their goals is to "divide and conquer." It is especially difficult for parents who are separated or divorced. Children will fall into the easy trap of manipulating the situation to accomplish what they want. Divorced parents must put their personal battles aside and work together in raising and disciplining children.

Like all parents, Kelly and I had disagreements about raising our children. We tried our best never to have those disagreements in front of the kids.

Tiffani once announced to me, "I hate the way you and Dad agree on disciplining us." I smiled and said, "I love you children. But, your dad was here first and he will be here last. You are passing on through to your own lives."

Parents do a terrible injustice when they tell children that they are the center of the universe and no other relationships matter. Such children will grow up ill-prepared for the tough realities of life. They will leave home with a distorted sense of self-importance and constantly struggle with the self-sacrifice needed in order to build future relationships.

Successful parenting starts with loving our children. It does not stop there. We must teach our children about God, provide for their needs and model positive self-esteem by accepting that our best is good enough.

Everyone Needs Help. Kelly and I are strong, independent people. Tera forced us to concede that some problems are beyond our abilities. It was so comforting once we realized we were not the only parents of a special child who had painful doubts and unanswered questions. Parenting is always difficult. It can be especially challenging with a special needs child because there are no easy answers, even to the easy questions like, "Can she put her socks on by herself?" It was humbling, and yet positive, for Kelly and me to admit we needed help.

No parents are perfect and all families are dysfunctional to some degree. However, no parent should physically, verbally or emotionally abuse a child. If you find yourself doing so, get help from friends, the family doctor, your pastor, a counselor or your child's teacher.

Don't Blame Yourself. Children grow up so fast. One night you don't sleep a wink because they are crying; the next night you don't sleep because they are driving! One day you blink back a tear and wave as they board the school bus for kindergarten; the next day you blink back a tear and wave as they walk across the stage at high school graduation.

Parenting is filled with joy and pain. Undoubtedly, the most painful experience is when parents give love, guidance, time and energy to their children and those kids turn out a mess. It isn't fair, but it happens. And, it isn't always the parents' fault. Children have free will and sooner or later they will choose to exercise that free will. Sometimes, the decisions they make are extremely destructive to themselves and others. When that happens, parents must not blame themselves. It can happen to anyone. Yes, it can and does happen to the very best parents.

I know some very good people who raised four children. The first three were so perfect that the parents could have written a book on parenting. The fourth child humbled them overnight. She got in serious trouble with the law at the age of nineteen and went to jail for thirty days. They refused to bail her out. They visited her daily, prayed with her and shared their love. They told her, "You have chosen the wrong road. We love you enough to let you stay in here. Use this time to decide if you want to make some changes."

While this girl was in jail, someone said to her mother, "I heard about Jane. I bet you are embarrassed." "Embarrassed?" responded my friend. "Why would I be embarrassed? I didn't teach Jane to steal. There was nothing in our home that told Jane it was an acceptable thing to do. She is an adult. She will be responsible for her own choices."

My friends were lucky, their daughter chose to turn her life around and become a productive, law-abiding citizen. Even if she had stayed on her ruinous path, her mother was correct in refusing to carry the blame.

We love our children. We do our best. We hold them accountable for their actions. And, we must allow them to be responsible for the choices they make. Otherwise, we deny them free will.

Fathers Make A Difference. I am grateful that Kelly has taken his responsibility of fatherhood seriously. Kelly has been a major influence in our children becoming fine adults. I wish all men were as dedicated to the role of parenting.

In America, the average father spends only ten minutes a day with his kids–ten minutes, how sad. It was easier raising kids when children worked daily with their folks on a farm or ranch. Kids knew they were needed. They arose with their dads, did chores with their dads and quietly bonded with their dads. Our fast-paced modern lifestyle has distorted that formula. There are now "commuter dads" who leave in the pre-dawn hours before their children are up and arrive home when their children are in bed. There are "traveling dads" who must be on the road for weeks at a time, missing ball games and birthdays. There are "absentee dads" who for a myriad of selfish reasons choose not to take an active role in the raising of their kids. There are "teenage dads" who impregnate young girls and refuse the responsibility of parenthood.

The job of being a father is exhausting, never-ending, time-consuming and too often unappreciated, but one simple fact holds true: kids need the love and influence of fathers. Successful dads can be quiet role models or bellowing drill sergeants. There is no one perfect style, but there are certain requirements:

- A father must love his children unconditionally. He must not love his children only when they are achieving because that feeds his ego and distorts their sense of self-worth.

- A father must have the courage to hold his children accountable for their actions. He must set boundaries and be as consistent as possible in allowing a child to fail, learn and grow.

- A father must make time. Everyone is feeling a time crunch and struggling to balance life's responsibilities. There will always be more phone calls to return, meetings to attend and paperwork to complete. No matter how full the schedule, a good father pencils in T-ball games, trips to the park, school concerts and bedtime reading.

Kelly taught our children patience, perseverance, discipline and compassion. He did it without sermonizing. He did it by example. Tera and Tiffani learned the importance of quiet time during the evening ritual of sitting at his feet while he braided their freshly washed hair. When a catcher wasn't available, he took Tiffani to the high school gym at six o'clock in the morning and daily caught 200 pitches so she could become the pitcher she wanted to be. He sat on the living room steps, listening to Troy practice his piano, because his presence said, "I'm interested." He patiently taught Tera to feed chickens and gather eggs so she could do chores like everyone else. He taught her to ride a horse when she became jealous because she couldn't ride a bike like her younger siblings. When she was struggling to finish a Special Olympics race, he left the grandstands, ignored the weight of his cowboy boots, and helped her complete what had only minutes before seemed like an impossible task.

Kelly taught our children to believe in God and in themselves. He did not do it in grand gestures, but in the little things. He cared, he was there, and he made a difference.

To Kelly and the millions of fathers like him who have helped little ones be all they can be, I say, "Thank you for carrying your part of the load." To the fathers who have neglected the job, I say, "It is never too late. Start today. Make memories. The job doesn't pay but the rewards are priceless."

Any fool can make a baby, but only a father can raise a child.

Mothers Make A Difference. To all the young mothers who are so tired they dream of twenty-four hours in a hotel room with nothing to do but sleep, I say, "Hang in there. It does get better. They do grow up."

To all the mothers of teenagers who are so frustrated they want to lock their children in a hotel room until they promise not to argue, complain and disagree, I say, "Hang in there, they will have children of their own some day and appreciate what you are going through. And, someday when they call you up and complain that their own children are being mean and rebellious, you can smile and say softly, 'Well, now, isn't that nice.'"

To the courageous, hard-working single mothers who have been forced to do the work of two parents in order to hold families together, I say, "Bravo. You are the true champions."

And for all of us, I share this poem:

Motherhood

It began with a twinge . . . a stirring

It grew in intensity . . . in purpose

Until my entire body cried against the strain

Until only God could carry me past the pain

and when my entire being said, "I can't—no more"

a miracle happened . . . my child was born

and my heart and my being exclaimed, "I am a mother!"

and God smiled and said, "Yes and it is good."

And the world said, "So,

it is nice, but does it matter.

Now your time isn't yours, you shan't be paid

and no one will thank you for dreams delayed

It isn't really important but for you we're glad"

and I doubted myself and God was sad.

But then bottles and diapers and toys filled my days
and she challenged my patience in so many ways
The memories of firsts were written in books
my heart held those firsts—the steps and the looks
and I stood by her bed and felt the stars shine
each breath in her body moved in rhythm with mine
A glow of love surrounded her face
Her presence told me of God's good grace
I said, "Oh thank you God that I am a mother"
and God smiled and said, "Yes, it is good."

and the world said, "Oh nonsense.
What you do for her anyone could do.
Is there talent in playing with paper and glue!
Is there skill in wiping a dirty face?
The world must be made a better place
and you can't bring peace to a world going wild
by loving and raising one gentle child!!"
and on days without sleep these words seemed wise.
I doubted myself and there were tears in God's eyes.

"Is it true Lord?" I asked when confused
"Is there nothing important in all that I do
Sometimes the days run together as one
I wonder if ever I had any fun
No more baby food, cribs, walker and rhymes
but home work and housework and job fill my time
I lose my temper, I regret what I say
please tell me Lord—am I doing o.k.?"

When Life Kicks—Kick Back

A slamming door interrupts my prayer
My attention is turned to the child standing there
She's been hurt, I can see past the pout
She walks to her room, shuts the door, shuts me out
I wait, I wonder, my heart feels a tug
quietly she comes, surrounds my soul with her hug
Her body feels tight, her tears tear me apart
she shares her sorrows, she opens her heart

There is such pain in growing up—I remember it now
I tell her she'll make it—I tell her how
The Lord loves you my child, you're his child too
If only you'd lived, he'd have died just for you
We talk for hours, we giggle and share
Her face slowly softens, she knows that I care
She needs time to herself now, she turns to leave
I call out, "You're special," she smiles and believes
As the room grows quiet and I sit alone
I think of how quickly my baby has grown
she loves herself and God, is alive and aware
and I have helped her in that by just being here
I know the world is wrong, I'm fulfilled and whole
The Lord stills the doubts deep in my soul
I love my life—I would choose no other
I am blessed—I rejoice—for I am a mother!!

Chapter Nine
Letting Go

Denial

parked in front of the medical clinic, opened the passenger door and reached for Mother's arm.

"Go get me a wheelchair, Tamara."

"You don't need a wheelchair. I will help you."

"No, the doctor's office is too far to walk. Go get a wheelchair."

There was no point arguing. I had never won an argument with my mother. As I assisted her into the wheelchair, I was reminded how frail and weak she was. She looked far older than her sixty-seven years. Her hair was unkempt, her sweatshirt stained and, as usual, she had refused to wear her dentures. Mother's lack of interest in her appearance was a strong warning that depression had decimated her self-esteem. I was desperate to find answers for her weakened condition. She had been to a general physician and orthopedic doctor. They had referred her to a neurologist for tests. Today we would be getting the results of the tests.

I could not navigate the wheelchair. I clipped the edge of the door and collided with the wall as we turned the corner.

"Be careful," Mother snapped, "you're going to hurt me."

"I didn't do it on purpose," I responded.

The elevator door opened. I bumped the back wall. I spun the chair around and the door shut on the wheel. A passenger in the elevator stared at me with disgust. I was embarrassed. "I'm sorry," I mumbled. This time my mother did not get mad. In fact, a smile crossed her face as she came to my defense, "Please ignore my daughter. She's a student driver." I laughed in relief. Mother and I were still smiling when the nurse led us into the doctor's office. When he entered, I introduced myself as Kay's daughter. He was serious and intense. He talked as if mother was not in the room. I found it insulting, as did she.

"Do you know why my mother is so unsteady and weak?" I asked him.

"Yes, I do. I have the results of your mother's tests." He walked to a lighted box on the wall and hung an x-ray.

"This is your mother's brain scan," he continued. "These large black lines indicate brain atrophy. They are in the area that controls coordination and balance. That is why she is so unstable."

"What does atrophy mean?" asked my mother.

"It means the blackened places in your brain have died because of lack of oxygen."

"Did I have a stroke?" she asked with concern.

"No, this pattern is consistent with severe alcoholism. Kay, how much do you drink?"

"I quit drinking," she answered firmly.

"Mother, how can you say that?" I turned to the doctor. "My mother is an alcoholic."

"Tamara!" snapped Mother. "I haven't had anything to drink for a month."

"That isn't true. You were drunk last night when I called."

"I was not . . ."

"It wouldn't matter," interrupted the doctor. "This damage hasn't happened over the past month. This damage is the result of years of abuse."

Silence hung heavy in the room.

"What can you do to fix it?" my mother asked in the soft voice of a child.

"I cannot do anything. The damage is irreversible." He paused, allowing the full impact of his words to sink in. "Kay, this is very serious. It will get much worse if you continue drinking. You are killing your brain."

Mother and I sat in silence after the doctor left the room. I was staring out the window, trying hard to control my anger. I wanted to shout at her, "How could you do this to yourself? I've been telling you for years to stop drinking."

My anger evaporated when I turned and looked into her large blue eyes. They were filled with fear. I gently hugged her. We did not talk as I drove her back to her apartment. I helped Mother up the stairs and sat her down at the kitchen table. She lit a long, thin cigarette. Her hand was shaking.

"Are you okay?" I asked softly. She did not respond.

"I must go. I have a two-hour drive home, and I am tired. Tomorrow I'll get a physical therapist to come by and help you. We'll get you a walker."

I laid my hand on her thin arm. She looked at me with a sadness that brought tears to my eyes.

"Mom, you know I love you. You must listen to the doctor. You must stop drinking."

"I will, Tamara."

"You can't do this by yourself. Please let me get help for you. "

"No," her voice echoed with stubborn resolve. "I don't want to talk about it now."

I kissed her good-bye and left. My heart was breaking. As I drove home I prayed, "Please God, make her listen to the doctor. Please give me the wisdom and strength to help her stop drinking."

I called Mother as soon as I arrived home. She was too drunk to talk.

Several months later I re-entered the medical building and walked to the same neurological office. This time, I was the patient.

"Did you get the results of my tests?" I asked.

"Yes, I did." The doctor's smile was kind.

"Do you know what is causing my dizziness and fatigue?"

He walked to the wall and turned on the x-ray light. "This is your MRI. These spots are lesions. I suspect they are causing your symptoms. I think you have Multiple Sclerosis. I would like to do a lumbar puncture."

"You mean a spinal tap?"

"Yes."

"Will it hurt?" I whispered.

"It isn't a pleasant test, but it might confirm my diagnosis."

"Might?" I queried.

"If the results are positive, we will know you have M.S."

"And, if the results are negative?"

"A negative report does not rule out M.S. It just means that particular specimen was inconclusive."

"I don't like those odds much. Besides, I hate needles."

"I highly recommend the procedure, but the choice is yours."

The doctor waited for my response. I processed the disturbing information he had provided.

"I don't want the test," I finally answered.

"Why don't you think about it for a few days," he said with a warm smile.

"I won't change my mind."

"I think you will."

"What makes you so certain?"

"Because you are a strong, inquisitive person, and you are going to want to know if you have M.S."

"I already know," I announced with an air of finality. "I don't have M.S." I left his office.

My mother and I were faced with the challenge of accepting or denying a life-changing diagnosis. Ironically, our reaction was identical. We both shifted into the detrimental process of denial.

Kay's Choice

I don't know why my mother became an alcoholic. Maybe it was because she loved my father with blinding passion, and he broke her heart. Maybe it was because dreamers are never truly happy. Maybe it was because alcoholism runs strong in her Irish ancestry. I don't know the reason. I do know it was painful to watch.

My mother knows suffering and rejection, but she also knows love. She has delightful, loyal friends. Her children try to make her happy. Harry, her second husband, cherished her. She was adored by her father and called "the duchess" by her brothers. Porky, her mother, revealed her devotion when she wrote the following poem:

KATE

At school they call her Katherine,
(it's an old Saint's name they say.)
Her daddy calls her Kathie,
and her girl friends call her Kay.

To her grandpa she is Kathleen
For she's Irish through and through
From her roguish Irish laughter
to her tender eyes of blue.

To her uncles she is Kitty
and her aunties call her Kit
But to me she is the taper
by which altar flames are lit.

She's the stardust in the evening
She's the dew of early morn.
And I know a thousand fairies
danced the morning she was born.

She is loyal and true and honest
and she'll toss a challenge to fate
So I called her for her Granny
and her Granny's name was Kate.

by Doris Dwan

I love my mother. I always have and always will. There is a tenacious bond between mothers and daughters that withstands time, tension and trials. We have shared marvelous moments and made precious memories. And that is why it is hell watching her kill herself.

I did not understand as a child that my mother was an alcoholic. I just knew that she was often volatile, fragile, and depressed. For as long as I can remember, I have mothered my mother. I held her when she cried and called the ambulance when she attempted suicide. I listened intently to her condemnation of my father and adopted her belief that he was the cause of all her problems. I accepted that she was a victim, and it was my responsibility to care for her. I defended her and made excuses for her behavior.

Like all alcoholics, my mother was a contradiction. When she was sober, she was bright, energetic and charming. When she was drunk, she was violent, irrational and irresponsible. She once found a picture of my father in my house. She threw the frame against the wall, shattering the glass and locked herself in our car. She honked the horn until the battery went dead. When my sister, Vallia, had her first child, my mother wallpapered and painted the nursery. Mother insisted on babysitting her week-old grandson so that Vallia could go to lunch with a friend. Then, she got drunk and passed out with the baby lying next to her on the floor. She did not awaken when neighbors, responding to the infant's cries, pounded on the doors, and shouted through the windows.

No amount of pleading and threatening could make my mother stop drinking. In fact, the neurologist's warning that she was killing her brain seemed to increase her determination to destroy herself. She rebuffed every attempt by family, friends and doctors to get treatment.

As I write this she is living in a nursing home. She is incapable of caring for herself. She is suffering from alcohol-induced dementia. She spends her time painting children's coloring books and staring blankly into space. She is a shadow of the bright, lively woman she once was.

My Choice

How did I respond to the doctor's diagnosis that I had M.S.? I spent years traveling throughout America and Canada in search of a more acceptable explanation for my neurological symptoms. I studied medical reports, pursued new diseases and squandered money on specialists and tests. Then I had an exacerbation.

"Tamara, can you hear me," the nurse's soft voice was far away, wrapped in cotton. "We are taking you to x-ray. We must do some tests. You are very sick."

"I don't care," I thought. "Just leave me in this peaceful place."

But I didn't stay in that peaceful place. I awoke to the frightening realization that I was in the hospital. I couldn't move my legs and my speech was garbled. Denying I had a serious neurological problem was no longer possible.

When I recovered, I returned to the neurologist. Once again he put images on the lighted x-ray box.

"If I compare your recent MRI to the one from four years ago, I can clearly see new lesions. The original lesions are darker and larger. Tamara, are you now willing to accept that you have M.S.?"

"Yes, I am."

"Good, then we can talk about your treatment. There is no cure for M.S., but there are changes you can make that will help us manage the disease."

"What changes?" I asked.

"You must slow down. And, you must try to eliminate stress from your life. There are also diets and . . ."

He talked. I tried to listen, but I couldn't focus on his words. My vivid imagination was in over-drive. "I have M.S." I thought. "Where will it take me? A walker, a wheelchair . . ."

When I left his office I was in desperate need of reassurance. I went to my mother's apartment to tell her the diagnosis. I rang the bell for a long time. She never answered the door. She was too drunk.

The two-hour drive home seemed endless. I was numb. Kelly was waiting anxiously when I arrived. I told him the diagnosis. He wasn't surprised. He gave me comfort and love. We went to bed and held each other tightly. Kelly fell asleep quickly. I couldn't sleep, so I prayed.

"God, I am so scared!"

"I know."

"What should I do?"

"Let go."

"Let go of what?"

"Everything."

"You mean the M.S.?"

"Yes."

"But, I don't know what's going to happen."

"No one does."

"Uncertainty frightens me."

"I know."

"And, my mother?"

"Let go."

"But, I love her."

"So do I."

"I want to help her."

"You can't."

"Why?"

"Because you aren't in control."

"Are You?"

"Yes."

"God?"

"Yes."

"Thank you."

I woke with a new determination to let go.

And, a luminous piece of the window was put into place.

The Lesson:

A ccepting my mother's alcoholism and my M.S. may appear as two different challenges, but they are one. They are woven together by my destructive need to control. They provided the ultimate opportunity for self-discovery and growth because they taught me to let go.

Letting Go of Control

I am a classic co-dependent. Kelly calls me the "Camp Counselor." I offer rides to stranded tourists, tips to confused shoppers and counseling to strangers on airplanes. It might be okay if my interference ended there, but it doesn't. I also try to protect loved ones from the painful consequences of their own actions and that has often been destructive to all involved.

Being a caretaker comes easily to me. It was the role I played as a child. It was a role that created conflicting emotions. The weight of carrying adult responsibilities was overwhelming, but it also created a sense of power and security. As an adult, I convinced myself that my co-dependency was motivated by compassion. I was wrong. Co-dependency is motivated by a need to control.

It is difficult to admit we have no control over the destructive choices of others. We are responsible for our reactions to them and the consequences they receive for their actions. We do not control their choices. Those individuals who are trapped in addictive behaviors pull loved ones into their pit of self-deception and anger. My mother stayed at our house the night my brother graduated from college. She was on a drunken rampage because our father had attended the graduation ceremony. She swore and screamed that she hated me. She threw things and slammed doors. No amount of begging or shouting could make her stop. I went to my children's bedroom to see if they were all right and overheard six-year-old Tiffani whispering to her little brother, "It's okay, Gramma just has a drinking problem."

I sadly realized that I was subjecting my children to the madness of alcoholism that I had known as a child. Later, I sent my mother a forceful letter saying I would no longer tolerate her abuse. I wrote that I loved her, but I also loved Kelly and my children. I pledged that she could no longer disrupt our home and if she got drunk and abusive, we would make her leave. Mother apologized and said that it wouldn't happen again. It did.

Loving someone with addictive behaviors is a roller coaster ride of hope and despair. People trapped in addictive behaviors expect those they love to exchange the reality of today for promises of someday. I believed my mother every time she promised to quit because I needed to believe her. I was my mother's keeper. Nothing she did could make me abandon her. In my heart I held on to the illusion that I could make her stop drinking. For thirty years I indulged that illusion of control.

From the moment of birth everyone is traveling down the road to death. Some people choose to drive in the passing lane. My mother is one of those people.

Her fuel of destruction has been alcohol. I willingly became a passenger on her journey of self-destruction. I finally said enough. It has been painful to watch her continue her journey, but not as painful as accompanying her.

Are you in a personal or professional relationship with someone who is willing to destroy you in order to indulge their own desires? You must accept the reality that you cannot control the behaviors, choices, and reactions of others. You must be honest with everyone involved. You must share your needs and expectations. If they then choose to continue their destructive behaviors, you must grant them the right to make their own choices.

- Walk away.
- The past is gone.
- Today hurts.
- You have a right to tomorrow .
- Seize it.

Letting Go Of Anger

When I was a child, anger was my protector, my friend. I would lie in bed and recite my mantra, "I will not trust. I will not love. No one will hurt me." Anger was an appropriate survival mechanism for a helpless child trying to cope with crisis. It is not an appropriate coping mechanism for an adult.

As an adult, I was still angry at everyone and everything. I was angry at my father for not being loving and my mother for being a victim. I was angry at my siblings, my husband and my kids for not being perfect. I was mad at myself for not being perfect. Most of all, I was angry at God for letting it all happen.

Unresolved anger deceives and corrupts. It initially makes us feel energetic and powerful, but it eventually dissolves our compassion and self-respect. My mother loved her children. Sadly, her love was shouted down by the bitterness she felt towards my father. Bitterness became her excuse, her comfort, and her master.

Tera was my mother's first grandchild. They adored each other. Mother flew to Montana to be with me when I was expecting my second child. The night I gave birth to Tiffani, my mother wrote the following tender words:

> Where is my child?
> I know she is grown
> But not to me
> My baby—My girl
> How can I share her pain?
> Oh Tamara—Let there be no pain
> Not for you—my special one
> You were born in early morn
> "It's a girl," they said
> through a soft haze
> "Are you sure?" I said
> "Are you very, very sure?"
> And so I was given, especially by God,
> a girl that only He could have sent

My mother was capable of being a generous, passionate person, until bitterness consumed her. Two years after she wrote this sensitive poem, she learned that I had made peace with my father. She mailed me a box containing every picture she possessed of Tera and Tiffani. She enclosed a letter saying we were dead to her. She refused to acknowledge the birth of my son for over a year.

Unresolved anger decimates rationality. There is a powerful saying: "Bitterness is like pouring acid on yourself and waiting for the other person to hurt."

Everyone has experienced cheating, betrayal and abandonment in their personal and professional lives. Healthy people acknowledge the violation, hold the guilty person accountable, and then move beyond the hurt. Unhealthy people become trapped in the injustice.

There are people who have everything they need to be happy: challenging jobs, loving relationships, good health. Yet, they get up in the morning and say, "I am going to give this beautiful day to a person I don't respect or like and let them trash it."

Are you thinking, "I would never do anything so foolish?"

Don't be so sure! If there is someone in your life who hurt you and you refuse to let go of the pain, then you are giving them each new day and letting them ruin it. They have gone on with their lives. Most likely they haven't spent one moment thinking of you. Yet, you have given them your yesterday and your today.

- Face your anger.
- Release the bitterness.
- Accept responsibility for your happiness.

Letting Go of Self-pity

The one word that most accurately describes M.S. is unpredictable. It is ironic that a control freak like myself is faced with the one disease that defies control. My reaction to the diagnosis of M.S. was predictable. I asked God, "Why me?" I should have asked, "Why not me?" Everyone has health problems. Athletic people have strokes. Healthy people have car accidents. Beautiful people have their appearance ravaged by cancer. Even the lucky few who escape illness and injury eventually experience the challenges of the aging process. As

173

my seventy-year-old friend Shirley said, "Old age isn't for sissies."

I once listened to a conversation between two dear friends who had lost children. Lisa's son had been killed in a car accident. Judy's daughter had died of cancer.

"I received that horrible phone call in the middle of the night," said Lisa softly. "I wanted to die. It wouldn't have been so unbearable if I could have said good-bye."

"It wouldn't have helped," responded Judy.

"Yes, it would have," insisted Lisa, "if only I could have held him and told him I loved him."

"No," Judy continued, "I said 'I love you' a thousand times in a thousand ways while my daughter was dying. Having the chance to say 'good-bye' was too high a price to pay for her endless suffering." Judy's words had become a whisper.

There was no point in continuing the discussion. Judy and Lisa knew that their situations were different, but their pain was the same.

We don't get to pick the challenges that enter our life. We do get to choose how we react to those challenges. M.S. forced me to evaluate my priorities and acknowledge my blessings. I have a loving husband, three great kids and special friends. I married into a delightful family who offered me genuine acceptance. My M.S. symptoms are milder than many people. I live in a free country. I am a very fortunate woman.

When I told a friend the title I had chosen for my book she said, "Do you mean "Kick Back" like confront or "Kick Back" like withdraw. I told her I meant both. Sometimes when life kicks us hard we must take charge and move forward. Sometimes we must back off and accept that we don't have control over everyone and everything. Always, we must trust God.

Giving It To God

I am certain of the following three things:

- Bad things happen to people.

- God could stop them.

- He respects free will.

Everyone will experience pain and suffering. Each time there is a crisis we lift our hearts to heaven and plead, "Oh God, don't allow this to happen." Sometimes God intervenes. Miracles happen. People recover from terminal illness, survive deadly accidents and narrowly escape vicious crimes.

When God answers our prayers with a "yes" we joyously say, "Thank you God. We knew we could depend on you." And when God answers our prayers with a "no" we cynically say, "You failed us, God. We knew we couldn't depend on you." Why does He answer some prayers with a yes and some with a no? We can speculate and theorize the answer to that age-old question, but the reality is, we will never know. God does not intervene every time we request it because that would destroy free will. Beyond that, we just have to trust.

A Sunday school teacher asked her kindergarten class, "What is God?"

One child offered a practical response, "I think God is a father."

One child offered a theoretical response, "I think God is love."

And one child found wisdom in simplicity, "God is God, and I am not."

When Life Kicks—Kick Back

Tera is competitive. She was running in the Special Olympics and she was in first place. Right before the finish line, one of the other competitors passed her up and won the race. Tera was upset. She looked at me and said, "Mommy, Kim beat me. I need faster shoes."

Tera speaks for all of us. Everyone feels overwhelmed by life. Everyone needs faster shoes. Each of us has whispered, "I can't do it. I'm not tough enough. I'm not smart enough. I'm not strong enough." Yes, you can, but not by yourself. Luckily, you don't have to. There are friends, family, doctors and counselors willing to help. There are angels. And always, there is God.

For the angels in my life who have helped me learn and grow, I have written this poem:

Fellowship

Our speaking stripped the armor.
The "self" awakened—alive!
Unveiling the hungry need
to become, belong, survive.
Self-worth so deeply buried
by pain inflicted at youth.
Blinders placed on by others
corrupting the view of truth.
The verbal self-discovery
melted away harmful myths.
Finding the me that could be.
Closing the painful rifts.
You listened with compassion.
You'd been there, I could tell.
You taught me self-acceptance
and walked me out of Hell.

God has made each person a unique stained-glass window. All pieces, dark and bright, are essential in completing the whole. The illumination may dim, but it never ceases. God not only wants our windows to endure. He wants them to shine.

When Life Kicks—Kick Back

PART THREE

The Final Lesson

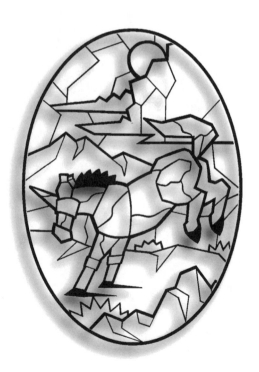

Chapter Ten
The Adventure

The pounding grew louder. It was powerful. It echoed off the trees, whipping the grass. Animals and birds spun around, *What wondrous creature is coming?* they thought.

Suddenly the unicorn burst over the crest of the hill. He was white and glowing as if energy moved with him–through him. The unicorn stopped and shook his great mane. The air rippled with each movement. The wonderous beast scanned the scene with eyes as blue as the bluest sky. The depth of the eyes was more dazzling than the color. All that beheld the great beast trembled.

Then the unicorn did a strange thing for one so powerful. He knelt down and with front legs bowed, the unicorn's great silver horn touched the grass. His voice, soft and firm, echoed through the valley, "Oh, great God who has created me, tell me what you wish of me."

"I wish you to observe my creatures and learn their lessons."

"So be it, my God. I thank you for allowing me to learn about Your creations."

"When you learn about them, you will learn about Me."

And, with that the Unicorn began his adventure.

He first encountered a herd of animals much like himself, yet smaller and without horns.

"They are horses," God whispered. "Join them."

He galloped with the horses across the open plain. He ran until the wind burned his face and his muscles ached. The horses did not care where they ran. It was the speed, not direction, that drove them. They barely slowed as they entered the nearby forest and soared over downed trees. Their muscular legs carried them across rivers. They leapt into space and flew down the side of a mountain. The exhilaration was empowering. He felt free. When the Unicorn broke from the herd, he was bursting with energy.

"Oh God," the Unicorn announced, "I see. You want the spirit to soar–to experience adventure–to know freedom–to leap forward, unafraid."

"Yes my son, you have learned a good lesson and now you should rest."

The unicorn found a soft patch of thick green grass under a great oak tree and drifted off to sleep.

His mane twitched. Something disturbed him. He lifted his head and scanned the horizon but he could not see what had intruded upon his slumber. He knew he was missing something. He felt it again. It was a tickling across his leg. He pressed his nose to the ground. There it was–a strange creature. A creature so small, he had to put his eye very close to see it.

"It is an ant. Watch it and learn," whispered the voice of God.

What could this meager creature teach me, he thought. *It is so small. It just moves back and forth.*

"Look closer," whispered God, "and watch."

So, the obedient creature laid his massive head on the ground and watched the ant. What a busy ant it was. It worked tirelessly, with great precision. It dug deep holes and carried sticks twice its size. It worked with great tenacity. The ant did not stop when the wind blew. It did not stop when heavy drops of rain fell from the skies. The Unicorn was enthralled.

"I see," he announced to God, "there is great satisfaction from focusing on a job and completing it. Your creatures cannot just play but must also work."

"Yes, but there is more."

The unicorn watched closer and this time he did not notice just one ant but thousands. They worked in cooperation with each other, and in perfect harmony, they completed a complex pathway.

When he lifted his head, he was surprised to see the sun was setting. He was more tired than he had been after his run with the wild horses, and yet, he felt strangely satisfied.

"It is clear," he told God, "they accomplish more together. Some are leaders and some are workers, but they each have a part to play in the building."

"Yes, my son, you have learned a good lesson and now you should rest."

And the Unicorn fell into a deep sleep.

This time the Unicorn did not awaken rested. He felt heavy. His eyes were heavy. His heart was heavy. The sky did not look blue. It looked grey. The grass looked grey, and it did not taste rich. He ate it because he knew he should but he had no enthusiasm for eating. The unicorn had no enthusiasm for anything.

He went in search of water. As he dipped his head into the cool stream, he closed his eyes and shook his head to clear his thoughts.

"Oh God, where are you?," he asked.

And for the first time, the voice of God did not answer. It left him with a strange uneasiness. He began to run as if he could catch the voice of God. He could not. Then he rested, hoping the voice would come to him in his sleep. It did not.

He wondered aimlessly. He saw the lessons of the previous day reflected all around him. He heard a high pitched shrill of geese flying together. He saw butterflies floating, free of burden. He saw lizards and lions eating, working, resting. He saw creatures of all size, but, he saw nothing new.

He lifted his head and with all of his strength he brayed, "What more is there for me to learn, God?"

His eyes were blinded by the glare of the sun. As the dazzling light faded, his eyes began to see two entangled branches. They were wrapped around each other as if climbing together. They moved. Strange. They were not branches. They were the necks of two giraffes.

A rustle in the grass compelled him to look down. He saw two fuzzy rabbits nuzzling their pink noses into each other's fur. From the corner of his eye he saw two robins bobbing heads together in deep conversation. He realized the large rainbow-painted butterfly resting on a nearby leaf was not one insect but two. And, for the first time, he noticed how many of the creatures were in pairs.

He understood he was alone and he hurt. With great effort, he lifted his head, "Are you there, God? Please say You are still with me."

"Yes." He felt the great voice before he heard it. The voice filled him with peace.

"Oh God," he cried, "I have learned the lesson. It is not good to be alone. All your creatures are unique, and yet, they are the same. They need to play, they need to work, and they need to be loved. Is that the final lesson?"

"No," said God, "that is not the final lesson, but it is a very important lesson. You are wiser now and it is time for you to feel what is in the heart of each creature."

"But, won't they all be the same?"

"No, I have made all my creatures unique. Each has a gift, and you must experience each gift."

The obedient Unicorn trotted into the forest seeking his greatest adventure.

A "hoot" pierced the quiet. He turned towards a majestic oak tree. An owl flew from a branch and perched on the tip of the Unicorn's horn. The Unicorn felt the wisdom of the owl flowing through him–sensible ideas–deep reflections–strange notions–frightening speculations. The thoughts were bright lights hurdling down dark tunnels. There was a powerful energy in thinking so many complex thoughts. He relished the power, the energy.

The ideas came too fast. They began to flow together. The lights got smaller, the pathways more confusing. He could not tell the sensible from the bizarre. The dark recesses of his mind were like an endless maze. The great beast became frustrated. Each thought ended with a question. He turned the corners in the maze and found a new idea and another question.

He felt trapped. He shook his head and the owl flew off. The unicorn was exhausted.

The unicorn walked slowly to an opening in the forest where he noticed a small lamb frolicking after a butterfly. He joined the carefree lamb, and with amazing grace the unicorn began leaping over flowers. He felt wondrous delight. He found himself laughing out loud. His senses were acute. The fragrance of the fields tickled his nose and created colors in his head. He felt alive.

He put his nose into a patch of golden daisies. An abrupt sneeze sent queer ripples through his muscles. A large bee flew from the clump of flowers and landed on his nose. Before he could shake it off, the bee buried its stinger into his soft flesh.

"Ouch," he wailed.

His delight was quickly replaced by distress. He glanced around for someone to console him. And for the first time he realized there was no flock. He became frightened. He laid down. He began to shiver.

The Unicorn no longer remembered the serious questions he wanted answered when he was with the owl. The pressure the owl had placed in his head was now in his heart. The potpourri of emotions he was receiving from the lamb made it impossible to think. He worried for his safety, and the safety of all others. He was overwhelmed with emotions: anxiety, melancholy, frustration. He felt such pain in his heart that he could not raise his head. Large tears of sadness rolled down his nose.

He sensed danger before he heard it. There was a howling in the distance. He knew he should run, but fear paralyzed him. He heard the growling. Closer now. He saw an eye staring at him from behind a tree. He saw the razor sharp fangs. He felt an involuntary shiver run the entire length of his body, and yet, he still could not move. He closed his eyes and waited for the terrible pain he knew would soon envelop him.

"Please," he implored, "do not hurt me."

He was overwhelmed with a sense of hopelessness and self-pity as he whimpered, "What have I done to warrant this?"

Slowly the unicorn felt energy pushing the fear from his veins. He opened his eyes. He was no longer with the lamb. He was watching the lamb from behind the tree. He felt no pity for it, only a strong sense that the lamb was a part of a bigger plan. He leapt onto the small animal and with swift precision snuffed out its life. He feasted and cleaned himself. He felt vital. Somewhere in the dark recesses of his mind, there was a hint of sadness that the lamb was dead, but that sadness was over-shadowed by a certainty that all things served a purpose. That certainty made him feel potent.

He stood tall and began to prowl the forest. He knew it was his forest. He saw no animals, but he knew they were there. They were in the burrows, under the branches, behind the boulders. They were watching with awe because he was the most powerful. He basked in the sun, confident in the knowledge that his strength gave clarity to the others. It gave order.

The warm sun relaxed his tense muscles. As he felt the tension float away, he realized that being the strongest also made him the most inaccessible. And, he felt strangely alone.

When the Unicorn awoke every part of his being was exhausted. His head throbbed from being thoughtful, his heart mourned from being sensitive and his body ached from being brave. He realized he had not spoken with God throughout his entire adventure.

"Where are you, my God?"

"I am here."

"Oh, God, it was the most confusing of all lessons. I experienced great gifts. I was able to think deep thoughts and dream great visions. I felt emotions so intense that they spread from my heart into my entire being. I was so mighty that my very reputation demanded the awe of others. It was amazing . . . but . . . I forgot . . . .," the unicorn paused.

"What did you forget?" asked God.

The unicorn continued, "When I was experiencing one gift, I forgot the others and that was the hardest challenge. It was very difficult to comprehend someone else's gift. Each gift isolated me. It happened slowly. At first, I had no interest in others because I was submerged in myself. Then I had no appreciation of others because I was so full of myself. Eventually, I knew only arrogance and loneliness. Oh, God, are these gifts bad?"

"What do you think?"

"I think nothing bad could come from You. But the gifts could be destructive if not used carefully. If we separate ourselves from others, our strengths will become weaknesses. Each gift is a blessing and a curse. Is that the final lesson?"

"That is an important part of the lesson, but not all. How do you feel now?"

The Unicorn paused before answering. He searched his heart, his head, and his soul. "I feel complete. I am not confused. I feel certain."

"Do you know why?"

"Because I have You."

"Yes, and that is the greatest lesson. I give gifts to those who can carry them. But, I know the burden is great, much too great to carry alone. Therefore, no one is alone. I am always near."

"Even when the gifts push others away?"

"Especially when the gifts push others away."

And, with that, a rainbow touched the ground in front of the Unicorn. The great beast walked up the rays until he stepped onto a cloud and disappeared into the waiting heart of God.

Appendix
Personality Inventory

he following personality inventory was developed by
Tamara Hall for use in her workshops and for individual use
by readers of this book. The material is copyrighted and may
not be duplicated without the written consent of the author.

Instructions: Please rank the following adjectives across each
line on a scale of one to four. Place a one (1) next to the word
in the row that best describes you and a four (4) next to the
word that least describes you. It is important to remember
that giving an adjective a four (4) does not mean you are
void of that attribute. It means in that particular row, the
other three words describe you better. Do not analyze your
responses or change answers. Stay with your initial gut-level
response as it will be the most accurate. Fill it out according
to the way your are, not the way you wish you were. There
are no right or wrong answers. Do all the pages before
totalling the results.

When Life Kicks—Kick Back

Remember: Every row must have a 1, 2, 3 and 4.

    1 = the word that best describes you

    2 = the word that second best describes you

    3 = the word that third best describes you

    4 = the word that least describes you

Personality Inventory

__fearless	__spirited	__practical	__tranquil
__firm	__charming	__factual	__modest
__self-reliant	__sociable	__obedient	__friendly
__pioneering	__extrovert	__accommodating	__tolerant
__competitive	__persuasive	__orderly	__hospitable
__willful	__popular	__precise	__loyal
__independent	__joyful	__accurate	__good listener
__strong-willed	__verbal	__efficient	__willing
__tenacious	__emotional	__contemplative	__trustful
__entertaining	__high-risk taker	__diplomatic	__lenient
__self-confident	__outgoing	__cooperative	__moderate
__determined	__energetic	__logical	__companionable
__assertive	__optimistic	__strict	__helper
__can-do	__exciting	__disciplined	__private
__defiant	__gregarious	__cautious	__empathetic
_____**Subtotal**	_____**Subtotal**	_____**Subtotal**	_____**Subtotal**

___impatient	___articulate	___dignified	___charitable
___decisive	___uplifting	___attentive	___thoughtful
___committed	___invigorating	___objective	___reflective
___industrious	___impulsive	___conforming	___sincere
___conclusive	___motivational	___soft-spoken	___compassionate
___definite	___whimsical	___compliant	___soft-hearted
___challenging	___imaginative	___methodical	___devoted
___forceful	___carefree	___systematic	___sentimental
___daring	___creative	___even-tempered	___spiritual
___bold	___lively	___cool-headed	___humble
_____**Subtotal**	_____**Subtotal**	_____**Subtotal**	_____**Subtotal**
_____**Subtotal** (pg. 192)	_____**Subtotal** (pg. 192)	_____**Subtotal** (pg. 192)	_____**Subtotal** (pg. 192)
_____**Total**	_____**Total**	_____**Total**	_____**Total**

Once you have completed the inventory, add the four columns on each page. Record the sub-totals on each page and total them. When you are finished you will have four totals. *The lowest score represents the one most like you.* The highest score represents the one least like you.

Column One describes the attributes most commonly associated with a *Taskmaster*, Column Two an *Enthusiast*, Column Three an *Analyst* and Column Four a *Mainstay*.

The strengths and pitfalls of each style are listed below. It is always fun to learn something new about ourselves, but it is important to remember that people are complex. Therefore, no single test can give us a complete view of ourselves. We are influenced by our personalities, values, intellectual level, circumstances and mental stability. It would be erroneous to judge ourselves and our potential based on this one short test. If you want more information on personality styles, there are many good books available at your local library and bookstores.

Column One describes the attributes most commonly associated with *Taskmasters*. You are confident, have a strong work ethic, take risks and are competitive. You show strong leadership and are politically wise. Decisive and logical, you are action-oriented. You value control. You have a tendency to be aggressive. Once you have made up your mind you have a tendency not to be a good listener, and you don't like compromise. You are more goal- oriented than people-oriented. You tend to be judgmental of others' faults.

Column Two describes the attributes most commonly associated with *Enthusiasts*. You are optimistic, expressive and courageous. You are a verbal processor. You enjoy today, are often impulsive and have a great sense of humor. A visionary, you value freedom. You would rather talk than listen. You don't like details and often lack self-control. You experience fluctuations in emotional highs and lows and have an excessive concern about social approval.

Column Three describes the attributes most commonly associated with *Analysts*. You are punctual, concise and logical. You are an excellent problem-solver and have a propensity towards math and science. You are reserved and cautious. You are proficient in learning new things. You value organization and intelligence. You are a perfectionist with yourself and others. You are not comfortable expressing your feelings. You would rather discuss what you think than how you feel. You don't communicate easily and have trouble accepting criticism.

Column Four describes the attributes most commonly associated with *Mainstays*. You are an excellent team player. You are sincere, empathetic and tolerant. You are the best listener of all four styles. You demand stability and have self-insight. You value acceptance for all. You do not like taking risks. You are not assertive or decisive and you don't nurture yourself. You value people more than goals.

**Tamara Hall,
M.ED, CSP**

Tamara is an international speaker who tickles the funny bone, lifts the spirit and challenges the conscience.

Her goal is to empower people to take control of their lives in spite of the high stress, technological changes and uncertainty of the 1990's. She does this with practical solutions wrapped in motivational stories and tied up with an abundance of laughter. Her top notch evaluations always state *"I've never laughed so hard or learned so much."*

Tamara is married and has three children. She lives in Bozeman, Montana.

For information on availability and speaking fees, please call 406-587-0590.

Order Form

Please send _____ copy(s) of When Life Kicks—Kick Back to:

Name: _____

Address: _____

City: _____ ST: ____ Zip: _____

Telephone: _____

Book Price: $13.95 (U.S.)
Shipping: $3 for the first book and $2 for each additional.
Payment: ☐ check   ☐ money order

Books $_____
Shipping $_____

Total enclosed $_____

Mail to: Communications Plus
         6734 Gooch Hill Road
         Bozeman, Montana 59715

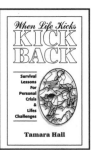

ATTENTION SCHOOLS, CHURCHES, ORGANIZATIONS, AND NON-PROFIT GROUPS: Quantity discounts are available on bulk purchases of this book for educational purposes or fund raising.